COLONIAL HOUSES

Modern Floor Plans and Authentic Exteriors For 161 Historical Colonial Homes

Edited by Home Planners, Inc.

Illustrations by Richard Toglia

A ROUNDTABLE PRESS BOOK

HOME PLANNERS, INC.

A ROUNDTABLE PRESS BOOK
DIRECTORS: Marsha Melnick, Susan E. Meyer
PROJECT EDITOR: Sue Heinemann
ILLUSTRATIONS: Richard Toglia

BOOK AND COVER DESIGN: Karin M. Lotarski
BACK COVER DESIGN: Design and Production Studio, Leslie N. Sinclair

PUBLISHED BY HOME PLANNERS, INC.
3275 W. INA ROAD, SUITE 110, TUCSON, ARIZONA 85741
CHAIRMAN: Charles W. Talcott
PRESIDENT AND PUBLISHER: Rickard D. Bailey
PUBLICATIONS MANAGER: Cindy J. Coatsworth
EDITOR: Paulette Mulvin

First Printing September 1990

Library of Congress Catalogue Card Number: 90-083504
ISBN softcover: 0-918894-82-4
ISBN hardcover: 0-918894-83-2

ON THE COVER: Capt. Obed Bunker House, Woodbury Lane, Nantucket, Massachusetts. Developer: The Woodbury Co. For an updated representation of this Colonial house, see plan J2103 on page 169.

TABLE OF CONTENTS

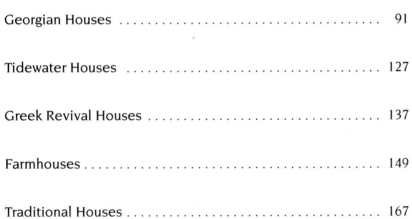

HENRY WHITFIELD HOUSE

Begun in 1639, the Whitfield house in Guilford, Connecticut was built for the Reverend Henry Whitfield, who had founded the town that same year. The house is believed to be the oldest existing stone residence in New England. The thick walls were laid up with granite that was quarried nearby; the mortar was made from crushed oyster shells. With its steeply pitched roof, massive chimneys, and small casement windows, the residence is distinctly medieval in design.

PERHAPS THERE IS NO STYLE of architecture with a stronger hold on the American imagination than the Colonial style. With their enduring designs, comfortable proportions, and practical materials, Colonial homes have a timeless appeal, suiting contemporary needs and tastes while recalling traditions deeply rooted in the past. America's settlers showed a remarkable interest in their domestic architecture, and as the country evolved from a struggling wilderness outpost into a proud, independent nation, many distinctive styles emerged. Still familiar today, these styles—ranging from the prim New England saltbox to the grandiose Greek Revival mansion—reflect not only diverse cultural customs brought from Europe, but also the way varying climates, geography, and economic conditions shaped a building tradition unlike any other.

This rich legacy, however, was hardly foretold by the inauspicious architectural beginnings of the English colonies. "Ther Howses are generally the worst that ever I sawe, ye meanest Cottages in England beinge everywaye equall (if not superior) with ye most of the beste," reported one Englishman, who visited the Jamestown settlement not long after it was established in Virginia in 1603. Indeed, both in Jamestown and in the Massachusetts colony of Plymouth, the first houses were nothing more than crude huts, dug into the ground and covered over with mud, turf, and branches. But the settlers were resourceful, and it wasn't long before these primitive shelters were replaced by better dwellings—essentially transplanted re-creations of the medieval farmhouses the colonists had left behind in their native lands.

EARLY NEW ENGLAND HOUSES

AS EARLY AS THE 1600s COLONIAL houses began to take on regional characteristics, as settlers of different nationalities established strongholds in par-

IRONMASTER'S HOUSE
Timothy Dexter, who was one of the original managers of the Saugus Iron Works, built this impressive Colonial house in 1636 in Saugus, Massachusetts. Its notable features include the peaked gables and the projecting jetty, or overhang, decorated with carved pendants. Because glass was scarce in the 17th Century, windows typically had small panes; the diamond shape is a quaint holdover from medieval England.

STANLEY-WHITMAN HOUSE
Built in Farmington, Connecticut, in 1664, the Stanley-Whitman house typifies the early Colonial timber-frame dwellings of New England. Such a house would be erected in a "house raising," in which the framework was assembled on the ground, then literally lifted into place. The central chimney and symmetrical window placement are standard for the period, as is the rear lean-to addition that gives this house its "saltbox" profile. An overhang appears over the first story, as well as over the second story on the gable ends.

PLYMOUTH HOUSE
This 1677 Colonial house in Plymouth, Massachusetts, is notable for its gambrel roof, which has two pitches on either side. Thought to have derived from English architecture, the gambrel roof probably originated out of economy; the "clipped-off" top required shorter rafter lengths.

ticular regions of the country. The northern colonies, for example, were populated primarily by frugal, industrious, middle-class farmers from southeastern England, and virtually every feature of their simple, functional houses was based on well-established English precedent.

Wood, which was plentiful, was the favored building material; stone was scarce in southeastern England, and most people from that region were not familiar with masonry construction. Even if they had been—lime needed to make mortar—was in limited supply in every New England colony except Rhode Island. What mortar mixtures were concocted generally proved quite unsatisfactory; in 1621, for example, while John Winthrop was building a stone house in Mystic, Connecticut, "There came such a violent storm of rain . . . two sides of it were washed down to the ground."

It is no wonder, then, that most houses were built of sturdy timbers, hewn from the trees felled as farmland was cleared. In New England the house frame was typically assembled on the ground—with the pieces numbered to go into the proper position—then lifted into place, one side at a time, with long poles. The assembling process, known as a "house raising," required the skills and strength of any neighbors who could be persuaded to help; the job was no doubt made easier by the knowledge that large quantities of food and rum awaited the housebuilders at a "frolic" once the house frame was completed.

Among the most familiar of Colonial styles, these early New England timber-frame houses have inspired the contemporary house style called garrison. Generally two stories high, they were essentially compact boxes, characterized by straightforward lines and simple facades, clad in shingles or clapboards. As warmth was a priority during the bitter New England winters, virtually all had a massive central chimney designed to heat the rooms clustered around it. Windows were small—generally either fixed in place (as night air was believed to be noxious) or casements that swung on hinges. In the early years, when glass was especially hard to come by, the openings were covered with wood boards or with paper coated in linseed oil.

A notable feature of many early New England dwellings is a projecting jetty that runs across the front —and sometimes the ends— at second-story level. The purpose of this narrow overhang, which might be embellished with carved pendants, remains a mystery. It is characteristic of 16th-Century houses in England, where it may have originated as a way to add extra floor space to the top stories of row houses that were packed tightly along narrow streets. No one is sure, however, of its function in this country; the feature may simply have been a popular decorative holdover.

The most common layout of the New England Colonial home was a two-room plan, with a loft or bed chambers above. One room, the "hall"—also called the "fire room" (due to the enormous walk-in cooking fireplace that dominated it), "dwelling room," or even "house"—served as an all-purpose gathering place, used for cooking, eating, sleeping, and work activities. The second room—the parlor, or "best room"—generally contained the family's finest furnishings, including the master bed, the most elaborate, expensive, and important piece of furniture in a household. Some houses also had a rear lean-to, which might be built as part of the original house plan or added later. This lean-to, another holdover from medieval England, provided space for a separate kitchen. Its sloping roofline, sweeping almost to the ground in back, echoed the profile of the boxes used to store salt, producing the familiar term "saltbox" now used to describe lean-to houses.

CAPE COD HOUSES

A FAMILIAR VARIATION OF THE NEW England Colonial is the Cape Cod house, which originated with the Pilgrims around 1670 and was commonly built

NANTUCKET CAPE *Located in a fishing village on Nantucket Island, Massachusetts, this* "full-size" Cape Cod cottage has weathered shingles on both its walls and roof. Typical of the full Cape, the door opens into a small central entrance, with a front room located on either side.

HADLYME HOUSE *Dating from around 1760, this riverside house in Hadlyme, Connecticut, originally served as a post office,* ship's chandlery, and general store. The steep roof, clapboard siding, and boxy design of the remodeled building suggest the feeling of a Cape Cod house. The lush landscaping, cozy front porch, and quaint picket fence are later additions which gave the structure a more home-like feeling.

© Julius Lazarus

BOW HOUSE

Due to its small size, this type of Cape Cod is known as a "half house." It typifies the many little fisherman's cottages that were built so extensively throughout coastal New England until the mid-1800s. The bowed "rainbow roof" is presumed to have been devised by ships' carpenters. Originally, the dwelling would have contained a single all-purpose room on the ground floor with a loft above for sleeping; the shed addition provided space for a separate kitchen.

throughout coastal regions of the northeast until about 1850. Small and snug, Cape Cod houses generally had only one or two rooms, often with a lean-to addition in the rear. Sitting low in the landscape, they have a boxy appearance, and typically are only one-and-one-half stories high. A particularly recognizable feature is the gable roof, which slopes down from the peak at a 45-degree angle, stopping just above the front door and multi-paned windows.

The little Cape Cod houses were generally situated to face south in order to take advantage of the winter sun and were often built on wooden sills, or horizontal timbers, instead of solid foundations, so that they could be trundled, or even floated, to a new location · if the sandy, unstable seashore site shifted or washed away.

DUTCH COLONIAL

AMONG THE MANY ENTERPRISING groups of Europeans to seek life in America were the Dutch, who founded the colony of New Netherland in 1626. While Dutch rule was short-lived, families from Holland and Flanders were allowed to hold on to their property and continued to live peacefully in southern Long Island, northern New Jersey, and the Hudson River Valley long after New Netherland was surrendered to the British in 1664.

In the 1700s the towns that grew around the fur-trading posts established by the Dutch became increasingly Anglicized, and few Dutch urban houses were built after the first decades of the century. Many rural farmhouses, however, continued to be built well into the 1800s. While these low, broad dwellings of wood, stone, or brick are now termed Dutch Colonial in style, they actually reflect an amalgam of building traditions brought together by all the various groups then settling in the former Dutch colony, including Danes, Prussians, Swedes, Walloons, and French Huguenots.

MARLPIT HALL

The long, low lines of this late 17th-Century house, known as Marlpit Hall, in Middletown, New Jersey, are typical of Dutch Colonial farmhouses built until well into the 1800s.

The steep roof pitch is medieval, while the slight flare of the front eaves is a hallmark of the Dutch style—although the exact origin of this feature remains a mystery. The house also has a "Dutch"

door. The bottom section may have been designed to be kept closed in order to prevent livestock from wandering into a house while the top section remained open to admit fresh air and sunlight.

Interestingly, the distinguishing feature of many so-called Dutch Colonial houses—a sloping roofline with flared eaves—has no known precedent in Holland and its origins remain a mystery. Numerous Dutch Colonial houses were also built with gambrel roofs, which have a double slope on each side. The gambrel, an economic roofing system also used by the English, developed during the 1700s to increase the roof span and provide more space on the upper story of the house. Still other Dutch houses have a simple peaked roof, often steeply pitched in the medieval tradition.

The interior plans of Dutch houses could vary, but, like those of the New England Colonial houses, they featured a best room, or *doten-kammer* (parlor-bedroom) furnished with a master bed.

THE GERMAN TRADITION

LIKE THE TOLERANT DUTCH colony, Pennsylvania—founded by the English Quaker William Penn— became a haven for numerous groups that were fleeing persecution in Europe. Among them were sects like the Quakers, Mennonites, Moravians, and Amish, who came from small, independent, German-speaking states in Central and Eastern Europe. Their farmhouses, built up into the 1800s and associated in particular with Lancaster County in Pennsylvania and contiguous areas of Maryland, display a mixture of Germanic design traditions. But because these colonies were English, the houses invariably incorporated English elements as well. It was not uncommon, for example, for a Germanic house in Pennsylvania to have a door or windows made in an English carpentry shop in Philadelphia—or to feature the popular 18th-Century Georgian floor plan, with a central hall and characteristic end chimneys.

HOLMES-HENDRICKSON HOUSE
This clapboard Dutch Colonial house, built in Holmdel, New Jersey, in 1754, was owned by the Hendrickson family until 1873. The so-called Flemish eave, which juts out over the facade, may be a unique and practical holdover from the "flying gutters" seen on cottages in Flanders.

CHADDS FORD HOUSE
Located in Chadds Ford, Pennsylvania, this substantial house served as Lafayette's headquarters during the American Revolution. It displays the sturdy walls of fieldstone that were typical of Pennsylvania German architecture. Other characteristic features include the projecting triangular doorhood and the deeply recessed windows.

WENTZ FARMSTEAD
The 18th-Century Wentz farmstead in Worcester, Pennsylvania, shows the influence of the Germanic traditions that prevailed in many areas of this mid-Atlantic colony. Among its distinctive features is the continuous pent roof above the first floor; a pent roof also appears at the gable ends at the second story. The walls are made of local fieldstone, accented with thick white mortar lines, and the paneled doors and shutters are painted in contrasting colors. The towering twin chimneys lend a solid look of permanence.

Generally, however, houses built in the Germanic tradition can be recognized by their solid and rectangular forms, often featuring thick masonry walls made from fieldstone. Dormers frequently protruded from the roof to light the second story; other distinguishing features included a projecting hood over the door and a long, narrow pent roof jutting out over the first story.

SCHIFFERSTADT HOUSE

The handsome Schifferstadt house, built around 1756 in Frederick, Maryland, features the center-chimney layout of the New England Colonial house, yet the masonry construction reflects German heritage. The walls, of rough-cut sandstone, are two-and-a-half-feet thick. The two massive chimney stacks serve four fireplaces that were designed to back up to cast-iron stoves—a typically Germanic feature.

COLONIAL VIRGINIA HOUSES

AT THE SAME TIME COLONISTS were establishing towns in the north, communities were also prospering in well-populated southern regions like the Virginia Tidewater. Whereas the northern settlers came primarily from one area of England, Virginians hailed from all over the British Isles, and among the Tidewater homesteaders were many skilled craftsmen, including bricklayers from regions in England where masonry was an established building tradition. Thus, while wood was still the dominant building material for Virginia houses, brick was also frequently used— particularly as the area offered a ready supply of clay for making bricks and oyster shells for lime to make mortar.

Like their New England counterparts, early Colonial Virginia farmhouses were simple and practical dwellings, often having a two-story center section flanked by low wings and usually containing one or two rooms on the ground floor. While there were various floor plans, it was not uncommon for the chimney (or chimneys) to be placed on the end of the structure rather than in the center (as was typical of New England houses). The end chimneys may have been designed to draw heat away from the rooms, a necessity during the hot southern summers. A central passageway running from front to back was also frequently incorporated to help channel cooling breezes through the house.

ADAM THOROUGHGOOD HOUSE

Believed to be the oldest house in Virginia, and perhaps in all of the English-speaking colonies, the Adam Thoroughgood house dates to circa 1636. Like its New England counterparts, this one-and-one-half story residence had diamond-paned casement windows and a steeply pitched roof. Unlike northern houses, however, the one-and-one-half story dwelling was built of brick and featured a center-hallway plan and substantial end chimneys—the archetypal design for Virginia farmhouses for the next century.

GEORGIAN HOUSES

AS THE 18th CENTURY PROGRESSED, a prosperous merchant class became firmly established in the New World. The early Colonial styles persisted in most rural areas during the 1700s, but the presence of Royal Governors in the colonies began to ignite a healthy interest in whatever fashions were currently the rage across the Atlantic. It wasn't long before the impact of prominent English architects and designers was felt in such sophisticated commercial centers as Newport, Boston, Philadelphia, and Charleston. Indeed, by the early decades of the 18th Century, the English Georgian style had made its mark on America, and its influence would hold throughout most of the century.

Because travel routes were well developed by the 1700s and communications vastly improved, news—and trends—traveled rapidly. Consequently, the Georgian house, whether the impressive estate of a successful New England merchant or the expansive plantation of a Southern cotton grower, developed a somewhat similar look in all the colonies. That look, of ordered symmetry, was firmly rooted in the formal principles of classical design set forth in the treatises of Andrea Palladio, a 16th-Century Italian Renaissance architect. Palladio had gained an almost cultlike following in Georgian England, where his work was widely promoted by architects, as well as in the countless publications then rolling off English presses.

No self-respecting gentleman was without several of these volumes in his library, and more than forty different architecture books, known as pattern books, were being used in this country by the time of the revolution. While some volumes offered sophisticated architectural theories, many were simple, inexpensive pocket-size carpenter's manuals, complete with floor plans and designs for facades, doorways, roof cornices, and mantelpieces that could be literally copied

MISSION HOUSE
The Reverend John Sergeant built this house in Stockbridge, Massachusetts, for his bride in 1739. The elaborate front door may have been adapted from a pattern book; the scroll-pedimented design is indigenous to western Massachusetts and reveals how the influential Georgian style made its mark.

MONTPELIER
This impressive brick plantation house in Laurel, Maryland, was built by Nicholas Snowden in about 1751 and enlarged with polygonal wings about twenty years later.

The stark symmetry of the design is a hallmark of the Georgian style, as are the pedimented doorway and the slightly projecting central pavilion, detailed with classical molding in white. The dual wings, projecting to either side of the main structure, were quite common. George Washington stopped here on his way to and from the Continental Congress in 1787.

TRYON PALACE

An impressive gate frames the entrance to Tryon Palace. Begun in 1767, the Georgian mansion was built in New Bern, North Carolina, for Governor William Tryon and was undoubtedly the finest house in the colony at the time. As no amateur builder was considered capable of executing a satisfactory design, Tryon brought over the English architect John Hawks to undertake the commission. The enormous palace was based on the plan of a Palladian villa and included a large meeting room for the North Carolina Assembly. The splendid estate burned to the ground in 1798, but has been entirely reconstructed.

LONGFELLOW HOUSE

Georgian houses in the northern colonies were more often constructed of wood than of brick. This 1759 clapboard-sided house, located in Cambridge, Massachusetts, was built for Major John Vassal, a wealthy Tory. The design is a beautiful statement of balanced elegance, with classic Ionic pilasters marking the corners and framing the elegant entrance. In the 19th Century the original house was enlarged by Henry Wadsworth Longfellow, who lived in it from 1837 to 1882.

HAMMOND-HARWOOD DOOR

The elegant doorway of the Hammond-Harwood House in Annapolis, Maryland, is one of the most distinctive in American Georgian architecture. The composition, incorporating a central fanlight, Ionic columns, and a crowning pediment, is enriched with carvings of festooned roses and ribbon-entwined laurel garlands.

off the page. As there were few trained architects in the colonies, these books proved particularly useful to the carpenter-builders who erected most houses. The influence of the pattern books can be seen not only in urban areas, but also in more isolated farming communities, where the designs, often scaled down, were interpreted in local materials.

Georgian homes, often built of expensive stone or brick, seemed to embody not only the wealth, but also the pride of a prospering nation. In both city and country, impressing one's neighbors was the order of the day. Frequently situated at the end of a meticulously landscaped driveway, the proper Georgian house featured a boldly massed design, sometimes marked by a shallow, projecting central facade section of rusticated, or rough-cut, stone. A centrally placed front entry punctuated the symmetrical composition and boasted a suitably imposing arrangement of columns and pediment, often designed as a full-fledged portico. Over the front door could often be found an impressive Palladian window, characterized by a central arch rising above elongated rectangular sidelights. A classically detailed cornice edged the roof, which might have a hipped, gabled, or gambrel profile. Windows were now numerous, designed with a double-hung sash and easily moved up and down.

Homes became larger as the century progressed, with three stories increasingly common. A greater emphasis was placed on brick permanence and crisp lines, replacing the florid carvings and sweeping curves of Early Georgian detailing. The chimneys—of which there might be two or even four—were moved to the end or corners of the house and a long central hallway connected the rooms at the center. The rooms themselves grew in number and now included a separate kitchen, dining room, bedrooms, and parlors for receiving guests, signaling a move toward specialized use and a new sense of privacy, which had been virtually unknown in the 17th Century.

HAMILTON HOUSE
The Hamilton house in South Berwick, Maine, is a prime example of the graceful mansions that were built by New England's affluent merchant class. The residence, de- *signed for Colonel Jonathan Hamilton in about 1785, sits high above the Salmon Falls River. Its hipped roof, exceedingly tall chimneys, and scroll-pedimented dormers are all features of the Geor-* *gian period. The simplicity of detail and the overall lightness of the design, however, show the influence of the Federal style, which was just coming into vogue at the time the house was built.*

MOUNT CLARE
The only pre-revolutionary mansion still existing in Baltimore is Mount *Clare, built in 1754. The central portico features classical columns on the first floor; the composi-* *tion is completed with a second-story Palladian window and crowning pediment.*

CARROLL MANSION
The Carroll mansion, of Baltimore, was built by Christopher Dresden around 1812. Its design displays the Federal style. The three-story facade is stripped of decoration, except for neatly inset panels, and distinguished by the rhythmic repetition of windows and dormers. The portico, with Ionic columns, is a statement of elegance.

PEIRCE-NICHOLS HOUSE
Designed by Samuel McIntire for Jerathmiel Peirce of Salem, Massachusetts, the 1782 clapboard Peirce-Nichols house is a combination of two styles. The solid bearing, massive corner pilasters, and pedimented doorway are all Georgian in nature. The squared-off facade, however, is simplified, and accentuated by the rooftop balustrade and proportioned windows, which diminish in size on the top story—indicative of the new Federal style.

FEDERAL STYLE

AMERICAN ARCHITECTURE AFTER the revolution was influenced by two related trends: a surge of nationalism that followed independence and a deepened interest in classical design, heightened by recent archaeological discoveries in Rome and Greece.

As the affluent mercantile class continued to burgeon in coastal communities, construction boomed, and with the new Federal government came what is now known as the Federal style, favored until about 1820. Federal-style houses were characterized by a refinement previously unseen in American buildings. Exterior designs became simpler, yet more elegant, with elongated proportions as the heavier massing of the Georgian period gave way to a graceful lightness. The box shape of Georgian homes was expanded in the Federal period in many instances to include wings, from the temple-form house shape. While classical detail still prevailed, the facades were generally very plain— perhaps gently broken into a rhythmic sequence of slightly projecting arches—and marked by an even repetition of simply framed windows. Now more elongated, the Palladian window was still in favor, as were circular and elliptical window shapes. The Federal house also typically featured a curved or polygon-shaped bay on an exterior wall and balustrade or parapet over eaves (rather than high on the roof). A handsome front door typically featured an arched fanlight above and sidelights. There might also be an elegant portico, centrally positioned to emphasize the classical symmetry of the overall design.

Often elliptical or circular in shape, rooms in Federal-style houses continued to become specialized, with elegant entrance halls, dining rooms and reception areas constituting the public spaces, while personal living quarters were moved to upper floors into the realm of complete privacy.

© Julius Lazarus

GREEK REVIVAL STYLE

THE 1820s MARKED YET ANOTHER new beginning for America. With the War of 1812 over, it was a time of peace and prosperity; the country regarded the future with a renewed sense of optimism. Embodying beauty, breadth, and permanence, no architecture seemed better suited to the national ideal than the splendid temples of Classical Greece—the earliest democracy in recorded history.

Mindful of their own recently gained freedom, Americans also looked on with interest and sympathy as the Greeks engaged in a war of independence from Turkey during the early years of the century. A passion for all things Greek soon swept the United States, and this in turn was fueled by the increased availability of publications with accurate reproductions of ancient Grecian ruins. Distant and romantic, those ruins seemed to evoke all that was just and honorable about that ancient civilization, a superior society with which America was eager to associate her own developing concept of civic virtue.

In its purest form, the Greek Revival differed from the Federal style in its far stricter adherence to the Greek—as distinct from Roman—vocabulary of architecture. Gone were the graceful curves of the previous era; columns were sturdier, profiles were squarer, lines were straighter.

As was true in other periods, the style was modified to suit particular needs, local

NANTUCKET HOUSE
With its characteristic ornaments and monumental proportions, the Greek Revival style was a splendid choice for a sea captain's mansion like this house. It was built in 1820 in the whaling port of Nantucket, Massachusetts. Four sturdy Corinthian columns support a massive pediment, forming the impressive "temple" front that is the signature feature of the style. Other classical details include the triangular pediments over the door and windows.

JOHN CALHOUN HOUSE
This mansion was home to John C. Calhoun, vice president of the United *States, from 1825 to 1850. Calhoun enlarged this residence in Fort Hill, South Carolina, during his ownership: a* *columned porch and Doric portico brought the house up to date in the fashionable Greek Revival style.*

materials, and personal preferences; countless variations were carried up and down the Atlantic seaboard, as well as westward with the expanding frontier. Indeed, no other style had dominated American architecture to the same extent. Every architect, builder, and carpenter in the nation, it seemed, tried his hand at his own version of a Greek temple. That temple might be as imposing as a marble-faced mansion fronted by a colonnade of Corinthian columns or as modest as a frame farmhouse on the Kansas prairie, painted white and turned so that the gable end suggested, ever so slightly, a temple front.

In all designs, however, there was always some reference to classical design, no matter how remote. Invariably the facade was crowned by a large pediment, which might be a full-blown design or merely suggested by a molding at the gable end of the peaked roof. The front door, sometimes in the center of the facade, sometimes moved to one side, was typically framed with pilasters (essentially flattened columns) and an entablature, or with sidelights and a transom of simple, square glass panes. On major houses, columns abounded, and if a house was not built of marble, it was painted white to look like it.

Room layouts also varied. Perhaps the most significant change of the period was the introduction of the double parlor, which ran from the front to the back of the house and featured sliding doors so the space could be divided into two smaller rooms or opened up for large parties. Innovation was greatly welcomed, and some houses were said to boast the newest of all conveniences: a bathroom, complete with tub, shower-bath, and water closet.

The Greek Revival, which prevailed until the time of the Civil War, represented the culmination of the classical expression in America. Lying ahead was the age of Romanticism, which would popularize an eclectic range of architectural styles. The Colonial period, by contrast, truly stands on its own, an enduring testament to fine design.

HERMITAGE

The Hermitage, near Nashville, Tennessee, was home to Andrew Jackson from 1818 until 1845. In 1835, after the house was damaged by fire, Jackson had it redesigned in the fashionable Greek Revival style. The Corinthian columns across the front were adapted from the Temple of Winds in Athens, creating a suitably impressive facade for the home of a United States president.

PLAN J2253

Type: Two-story
Style: Garrison
First floor: 1,501 square feet
Second floor: 1,291 square feet
Total: 2,792 square feet
Bedrooms: 3
Bathrooms: 2½
Price schedule: C

Medieval design elements, diamond-pane windows, second-story overhang, and a large central chimney hint at the origins of this garrison-style Colonial. The floor plan, however, reflects today's lifestyle. Highlights include an ample living room, kitchen with a convenient eating nook, and a family room with a fireplace. Little extras add to this design's appeal — the large fireplaces, built-in bookshelves in the living room and dining room, the wet bar in the family room. Notice the abundant closet space throughout the upstairs.

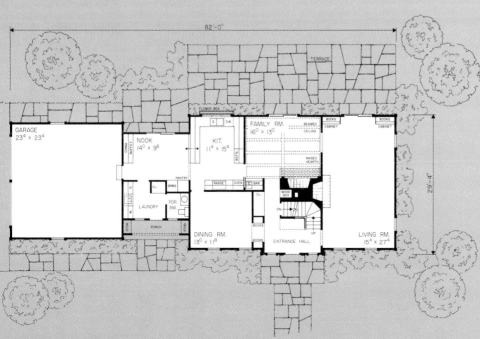

PLAN J2398

Type: Two-story
Style: Garrison
First floor: 1,572 square feet
Second floor: 1,008 square feet
Total: 2,580 square feet
Bedrooms: 4
Bathrooms: 2½
Price schedule: B

This plan features a twist on the central-hall design with its first floor bedroom. Alternatively, this room could function as a den or study. Notice the large family room with beamed ceiling and massive fireplace — perfect for relaxing.

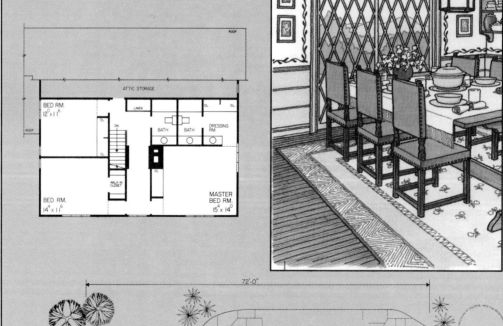

The sliding door in the dining room bathes the room in light and affords a nice view of the back yard.

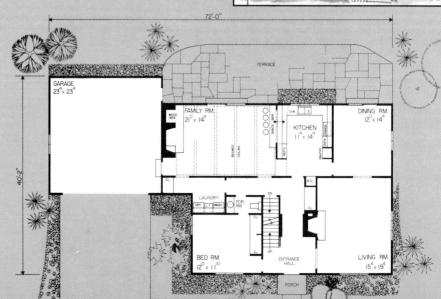

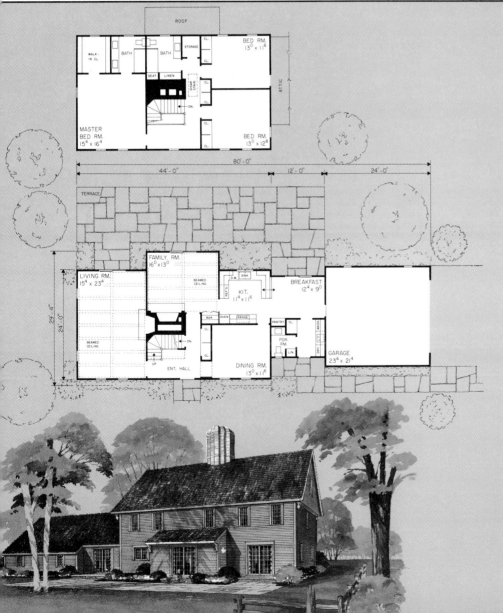

PLAN J2101

Type: Two-story
Style: Garrison
First floor: 1,338 square feet
Second floor: 1,114 square feet
Total: 2,452 square feet
Bedrooms: 3
Bathrooms: 2½
Price schedule: B

The spacious back terrace makes this home perfect for families who enjoy outdoor living. Large doors and windows let the sun shine in, bringing the outside indoors. The spacious interior combines Colonial detail and modern livability. Both the living room and family room have beamed ceilings and large fireplaces. The modern U-shaped kitchen has an adjacent breakfast room overlooking the back yard. There's also a bar in the family room. Notice the closet space in upstairs bedrooms.

PLAN J2692

Type: Two-story
Style: Garrison
First floor: 1,965 square feet with greenhouse
Second floor: 1,395 square feet
Total: 3,360
Bedrooms: 4
Bathrooms: 2½
Price schedule: C

Diamond-pane windows enhance the traditional exterior of this Colonial. Inside, the floor plan departs from convention with a greenhouse, country kitchen, and clutter room. Upstairs are four bedrooms; the master even has a fireplace.

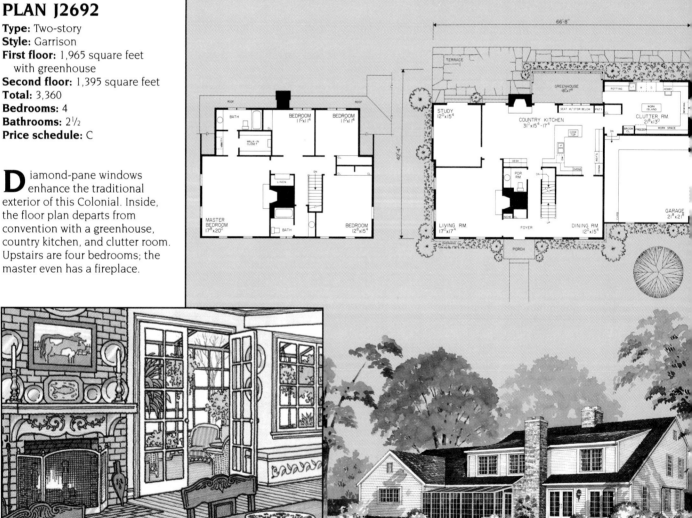

The large country kitchen has an entrance to the greenhouse.

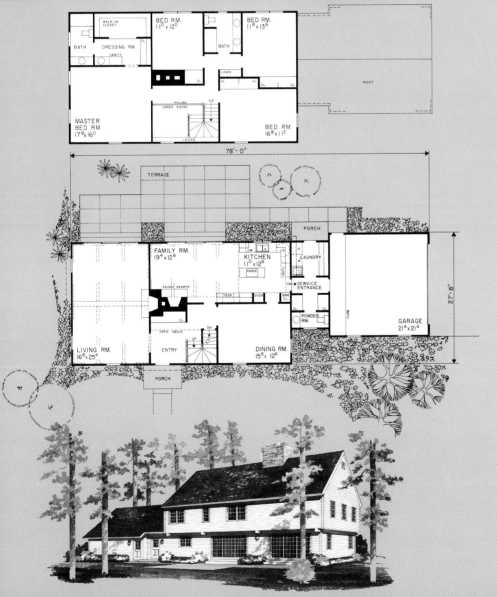

PLAN J2651

Type: Two-story
Style: Garrison
First floor: 1,404 square feet
Second floor: 1,323 square feet
Total: 2,727 square feet
Bedrooms: 4
Bathrooms: 2½
Price schedule: C

Featuring a large living room which stretches to the rear of the house, this home seems to be designed for entertaining. The terrace, adjacent to both the living room and family room, provides a spot for outdoor gatherings. The open family room and kitchen create an informal area where the family can relax and work together. Upstairs are four bedrooms; the master boasts a walk-in closet and dressing room. Don't miss the storage space in the garage.

PLAN J2191

Type: Two-story
Style: Garrison
First floor: 1,553 square feet
Second floor: 1,197 square feet
Total: 2,750 square feet
Bedrooms: 3
Bathrooms: 2½
Price schedule: C

The distinctive gables make this garrison-style home stand out from the rest. Inside, the beamed-ceilinged living and family rooms continue the Early American theme. Also notice the large fireplaces. The efficient, U-shaped kitchen and nook overlook the back yard. The three-bedroom upstairs includes a lounge with a window seat. Don't miss the built-in china shelves in the dining room.

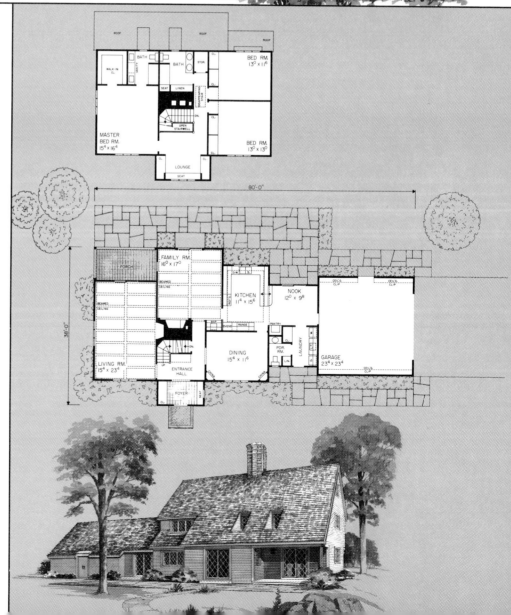

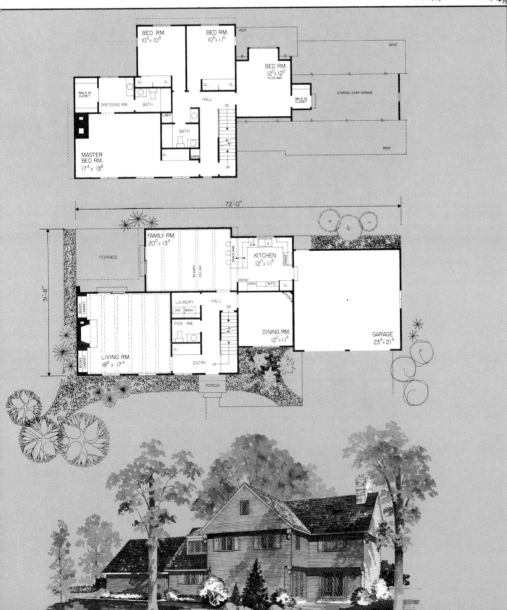

PLAN J2642

Type: Two-story
Style: Garrison
First floor: 1,222 square feet
Second floor: 1,233 square feet
Total: 2,455 square feet
Bedrooms: 4
Bathrooms: 2½
Price schedule: B

Here is a house with plenty of history. Without the side appendages, it is reminiscent of Boston's Paul Revere House, built c. 1676. Its interior, however, belongs to the 20th Century. This plan features both a living room and family room. The living room fireplace is flanked by built-in bookshelves. A snack bar pass-through joins the kitchen and family room, creating a space where the family can work and relax together. Also notice the four-bedroom upstairs with its two full baths.

PLAN J1719

Type: Two-story
Style: Garrison
First floor: 864 square feet
Second floor: 896 square feet
Total: 1,760 square feet
Bedrooms: 4
Bathrooms: 2½
Price schedule: A

Like original Colonial houses, this plan is built around a central chimney and staircase, which eliminates wasted hall space. Highlights of this design include a U-shaped kitchen open to the family room and four bedrooms upstairs. All elements mesh together to make this a compact, hard-working plan.

The living room fireplace creates a cozy corner.

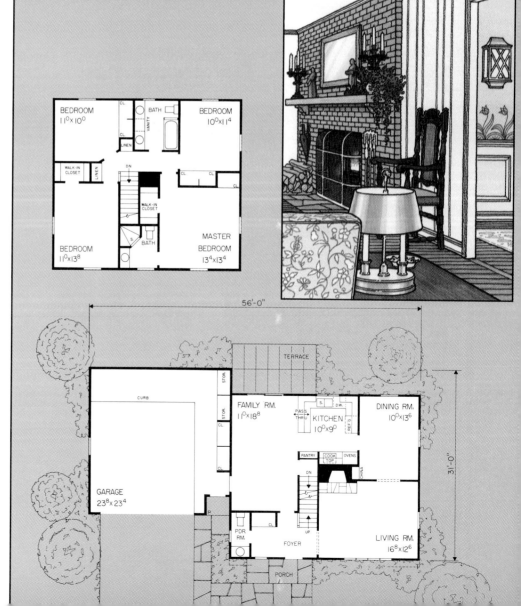

PLAN J2666

Type: Two-story
Style: Garrison
First floor: 988 square feet
Second floor: 1,147 square feet
Total: 2,135 square feet
Bedrooms: 4
Bathrooms: 2½
Price schedule: B

A sensible, livable floor plan highlights the interior of this design. The spacious country kitchen includes a convenient island work center. There's a raised-hearth fireplace to gather around and space for an eating nook. The side entrance will make quick work of unloading groceries. Also downstairs are the living room with fireplace and formal dining room. Sliding doors in the living room and kitchen allow for outdoor living and entertaining. Upstairs are four bedrooms; the master bedroom features a large walk-in closet and private bath. Also notice the closet space throughout the house.

25

PLAN J2305

Type: Two-story
Style: Garrison
First floor: 1,373 square feet
Second floor: 1,452 square feet
Total: 2,825 square feet
Bedrooms: 4
Bathrooms: 3½
Price schedule: C

Diamond-pane bay windows highlight the exterior of this central-hall garrison. Inside, the gracious entrance hall leads to the formal dining room and beamed-ceilinged living room with fireplace. The adjacent porch provides a shaded spot for relaxing in warm weather. The efficient U-shaped kitchen has a breakfast nook. To the rear is the sunken family room. The rear porch provides sheltered access to the garage. Four bedrooms upstairs round out the plan. Also notice the attic storage.

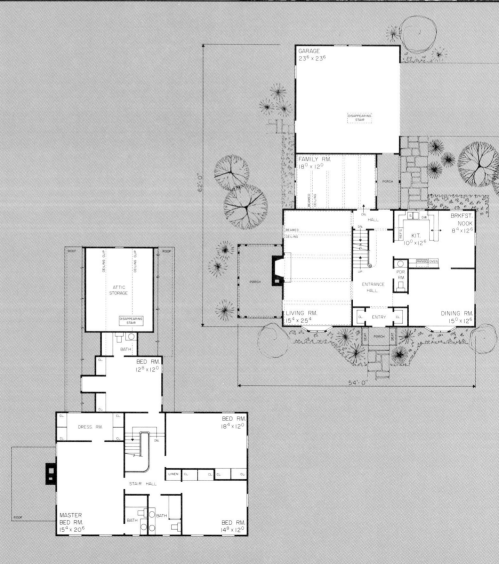

PLAN J2322

Type: Two-story
Style: Garrison
First floor: 1,480 square feet,
Second floor: 1,172 square feet
Total: 2,652 square feet
Bedrooms: 5
Bathrooms: 2½
Price schedule: B

A good choice for large families, this design has five bedrooms upstairs. There's plenty of living space on the first floor with a large living room and family room, both with fireplaces. An ample kitchen with an eating nook is convenient to the dining room and family room. The dining room has a bay window overlooking the back yard. A cozy study with built-in bookshelves beckons those looking for a quiet place to work. Also notice the abundant closet space throughout the plan and the curbed storage area in the garage.

BED RM.
12⁰ x 12⁰

BED RM.
10⁸ x 10⁰

BATH   BATH

DRESS
RM.

LIN.   CL.

CL.   CL.

DN.   CL.

CL.   CL.

BED RM.
13⁶ x 11⁸

BED RM.
11⁸ x 9⁴

MASTER
BED RM.
13⁶ x 15⁰

ROOF

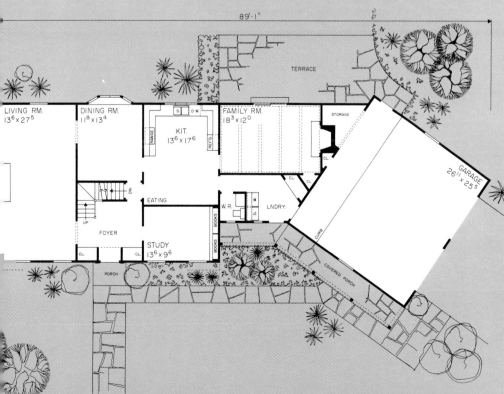

89'-1"

TERRACE

LIVING RM.
13⁶ x 27⁵

DINING RM.
11⁸ x 13⁴

KIT.
13⁶ x 17⁶

FAMILY RM.
18³ x 12⁰

STORAGE

RANGE   REF'G.

S   D.W.

CL.   CL.

GARAGE
26¹¹ x 25⁵

EATING

W.R.   LNDRY.

D.

CURB

UP   DN.

FOYER

STUDY
13⁶ x 9⁶

BOOKS   BOOKS

CL.   CL.

COVERED PORCH

PORCH

PLAN J1266

Type: Two-story
Style: Garrison
First floor: 1,374 square feet
Second floor: 1,094 square feet
Total: 2,468 square feet
Bedrooms: 5
Bathrooms: 3
Price schedule: B

Typical of the Garrison style, this home features multi-paned windows, massive central chimney, and overhanging second story which has its roots in medieval English architectural styles. Inside, a special feature of this plan is its first floor bedroom which may also serve as a study, depending on your family's needs. Also noteworthy are the living room with fireplace, the kitchen open to the family room, and a spacious back terrace with access from both the dining room and family room. The second floor features four good-sized bedrooms, two full baths, and abundant closet space.

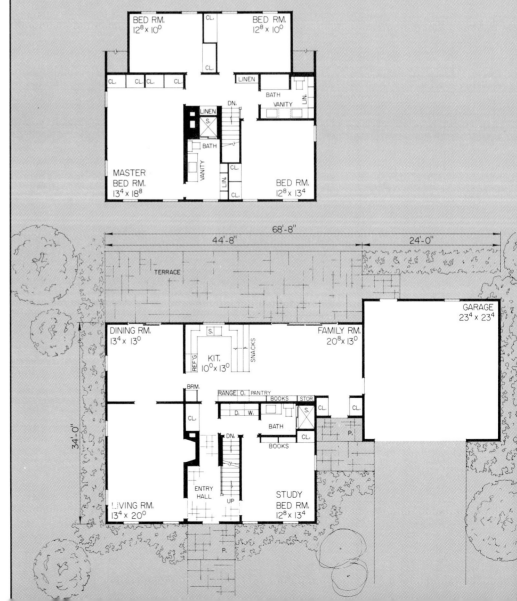

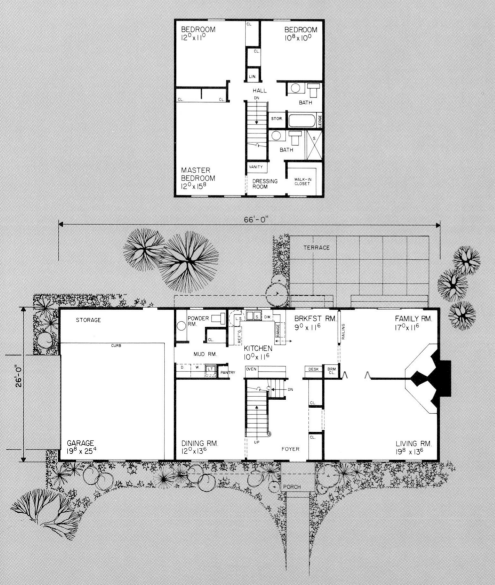

PLAN J2799

Type: Two-story
Style: Garrison
First floor: 1,196 square feet
Second floor: 780 square feet
Total: 1,976 square feet
Bedrooms: 3
Bathrooms: 2½
Price schedule: A

Floor-to-ceiling windows in this home put a twist on traditional Colonial facades. This adaptation features symmetrical wings, one housing the garage, the other containing the living and family rooms. The living room and family room both boast corner fireplaces. The kitchen with breakfast room connects with the dining room and family room for easy serving of meals and snacks. The mud room leading to the garage has space for a washer and dryer. Upstairs are three bedrooms including a master with a dressing room and walk-in closet.

PLAN J1849

Type: Two-story
Style: Garrison
First floor: 1,008 square feet
Second floor: 1,080 square feet
Total: 2,088 square feet
Bedrooms: 5
Bathrooms: 2½
Price schedule: B

This garrison-type adaptation projects all the romance of yesteryear. The narrow, horizontal siding, the window detailing, and the overhanging second floor with its carved pendant drops help set this home apart. Just off the entry hall, the beamed-ceilinged family room will be an inviting place to gather. There's a pass-through to the kitchen for easy serving. A dining room and living room with a fireplace round out the first floor. Upstairs are five bedrooms and two full baths.

The living room fireplace has a convenient built-in wood box.

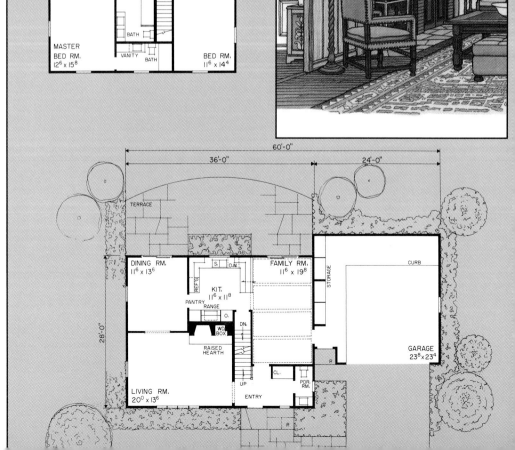

PLAN J2653

Type: Two-story
Style: Saltbox
First floor: 2,016 square feet
Second floor: 1,656 square feet
Total: 3,672 square feet
Bedrooms: 4 + library
Bathrooms: 2½
Price schedule: C

This distinctive saltbox has nine-over-nine windows on the ground floor and a pedimented front porch. Inside highlights include a mammoth living room with beamed ceilings, a spacious dining room, and a corner library. Be sure to notice the extensive built-in storage space in the dining room. The U-shaped kitchen features an island work center and a pass-through to the beamed-ceilinged family room. There's also a full service area next to the garage. Upstairs are four bedrooms, one of which could serve as a study. Take special note of the fireplace in the master bedroom.

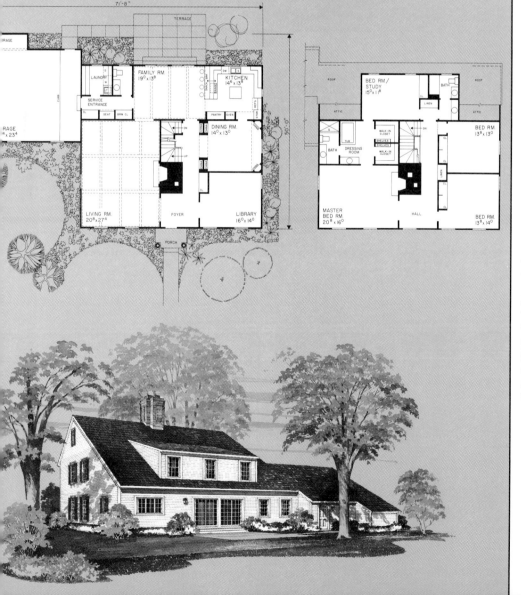

PLAN J2399

Type: Two-story
Style: Saltbox
First floor: 1,301 square feet
Second floor: 839 square feet
Total: 2,140 square feet
Bedrooms: 3
Bathrooms: 3
Price schedule: B

This design boasts a simple, clean-lined exterior and a livable floor plan. The beamed-ceilinged gathering room has a raised-hearth fireplace and two sliding glass doors onto a terrace. There's also space for a dining area, if you choose. The adjacent kitchen has an eating nook and overlooks the back yard. Also downstairs is a bedroom and full bath, a perfect arrangement for guests. Upstairs are two more bedrooms and full baths plus extra space in the stair hall for a small sitting area.

The open, winding staircase makes for a gracious entrance hall.

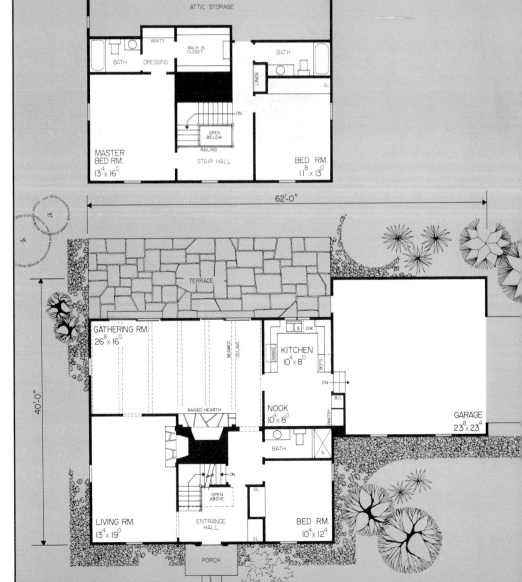

PLAN J2731

Type: Two-story
Style: Saltbox
First floor: 1,039 square feet
Second floor: 973 square feet
Total: 2,012 square feet
Bedrooms: 3 + study
Bathrooms: 2½
Price schedule: B

Enormous multi-pane windows let plenty of sun into this handsome saltbox. A bay window and sliding glass door make the kitchen a bright, cheery place. Other highlights include a living room with a fireplace and a downstairs study.

A bay with five windows overlooks the backyard and terrace.

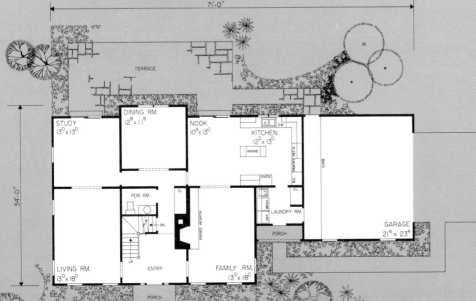

PLAN J2538

Type: Two-story
Style: Saltbox
First floor: 1,503 square feet
Second floor: 1,095 square feet
Total: 2,598 square feet
Bedrooms: 4 + study
Bathrooms: 2½
Price schedule: B

Flanking the two-story entry are the living room and family room with raised-hearth fireplace. The kitchen with its cooking island and spacious eating nook, the dining room and a corner study complete the first floor. Four bedrooms are upstairs; be sure to notice the fireplace in the master suite.

An open, angled staircase graces the large entrance.

35

PLAN J1900

Type: Two-story
Style: Saltbox
First floor: 1,672 square feet
Second floor: 1,287 square feet
Total: 2,959 square feet
Bedrooms: 5
Bathrooms: 3
Price schedule: C

Two entrances separate formal and informal living zones in this plan. The front door leads to the formal living room, dining room, and guest room while the mud room entrance connects with the family room and kitchen. Note the fireplace in the family room.

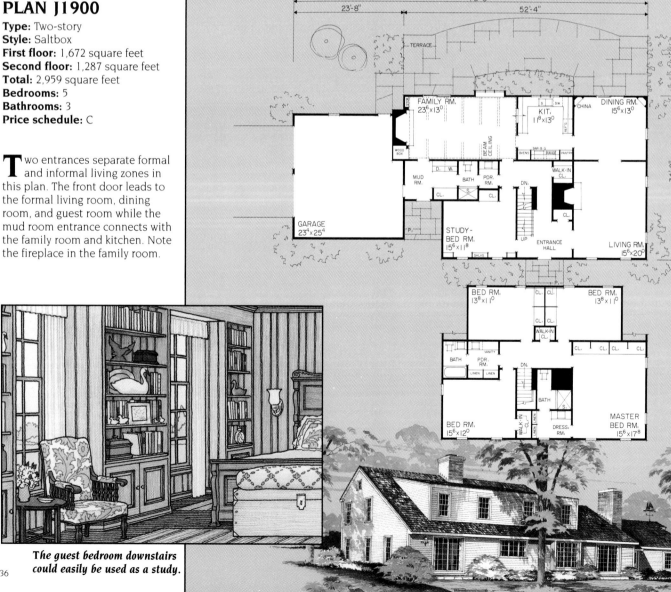

The guest bedroom downstairs could easily be used as a study.

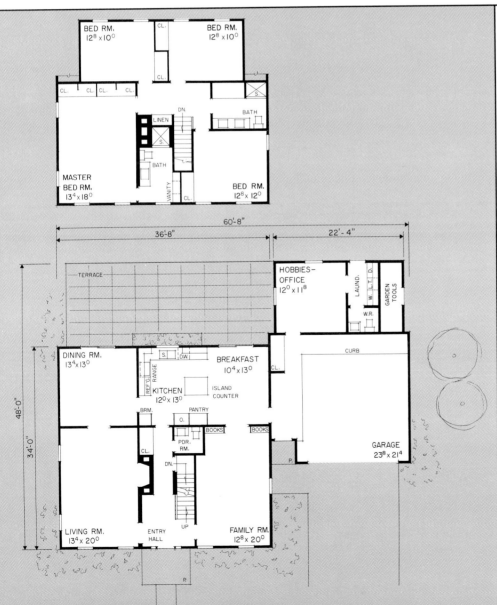

PLAN J1814

Type: Two-story
Style: Saltbox
First floor: 1,471 square feet including hobby extension
Second floor: 1,052 square feet
Total: 2,523 square feet
Bedrooms: 4 + hobby room
Bathrooms: 2½ + powder room
Price schedule: B

This spacious center-hall Colonial features a practical, livable floor plan. A living room with a fireplace leads into the dining room and kitchen, which boasts an island counter and a large breakfast area. A handy hobby room/office and laundry are conveniently located behind the garage. Upstairs are four bedrooms, two full baths, and plenty of closet space.

PLAN J2654

Type: Two-story
Style: Saltbox
First floor: 1,152 square feet
Second floor: 844 square feet
Total: 1,996 square feet
Bedrooms: 3 + study
Bathrooms: 2½
Price schedule: A

A cheerful flower garden out front welcomes visitors to this center-hall saltbox. Flanking the foyer are the living room and study with built-in shelving. The spacious kitchen opens onto the rear terrace. Garden storage is located behind the garage.

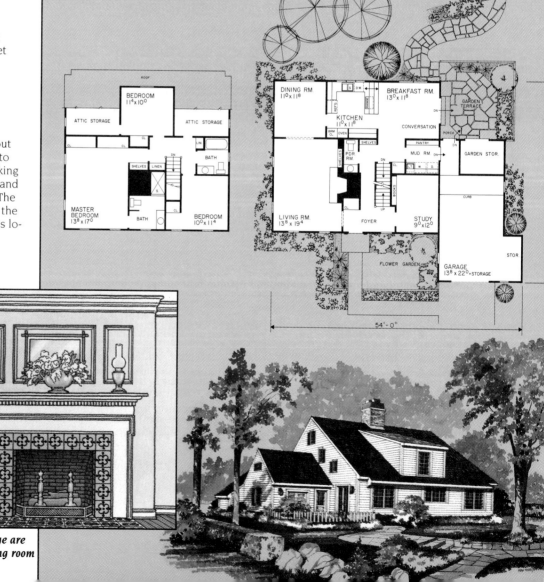

Built-in shelves for storage are located alongside the living room fireplace.

PLAN J1142

Type: Two-story
Style: Saltbox
First floor: 1,525 square feet
Second floor: 1,053 square feet
with fourth bedroom
Total: 2,578 square feet
Bedrooms: 3 or 4 (study)
Bathrooms: 3
Price schedule: B

This home includes several options for growing families. The upstairs features either a three- or four-bedroom plan while the first floor includes a study/bedroom with its own full bath. Also downstairs, the living room, dining room, and open kitchen and family room provide plenty of living space, even for large families. The enormous family room has enough space to serve many functions; there's room for an informal eating area in addition to the snack bar and a relaxing area by the raised-hearth fireplace. Also notice the window seat — perfect for curling up with a book.

PLAN J2616

Type: Two-story
Style: Saltbox
First floor: 1,415 square feet
Second floor: 1,106 square feet
Total: 2,521 square feet
Bedrooms: 4
Bathrooms: 2½
Price schedule: B

The extras in this plan make for a livable, comfortable home: Three fireplaces downstairs provide warm, cozy spaces for working and relaxing. The kitchen features a beamed-ceilinged breakfast room with a sliding glass door onto the terrace. Upstairs are four bedrooms.

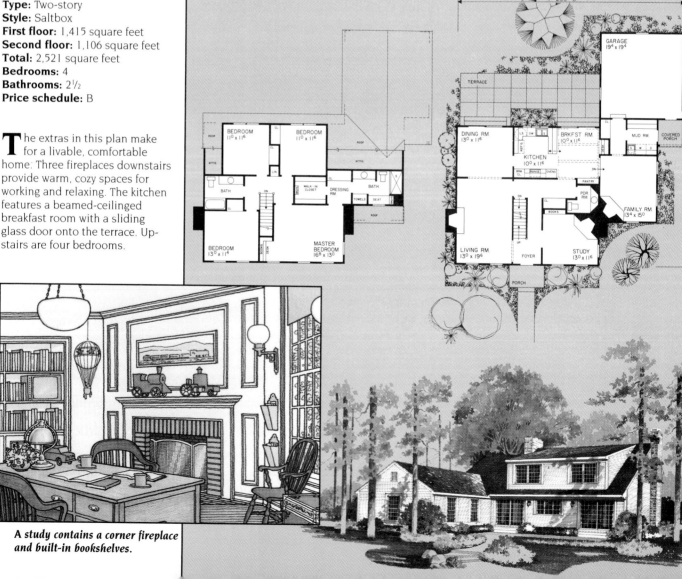

A study contains a corner fireplace and built-in bookshelves.

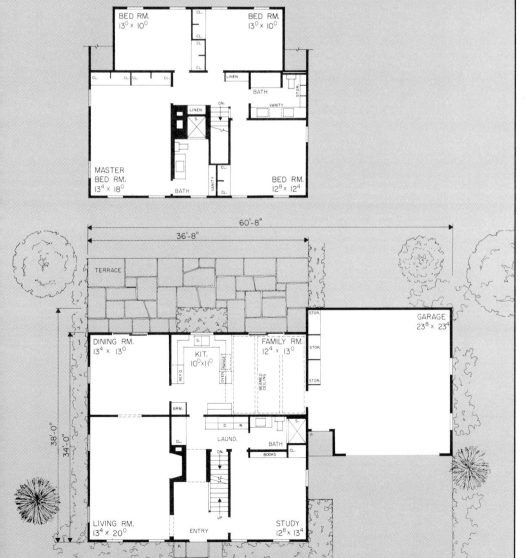

PLAN J1202

Type: Two-story
Style: Saltbox
First floor: 1,246 square feet
Second floor: 1,052 square feet
Total: 2,298 square feet
Bedrooms: 4 or 5 (study)
Bathrooms: 3
Price schedule: B

Shuttered, multi-pane windows adorn the simple facade of this saltbox. This home is carefully zoned for utmost livability. The living room leads into the formal dining room which connects with the kitchen. The study is placed at the front of the plan, away from the bustle and noise of the kitchen and family room. The kitchen is located next to the dining room and family room for convenient serving of meals and snacks. Upstairs are four nice-sized bedrooms and two full baths. Notice the abundant closet space throughout the house.

PLAN J2623

Type: Two-story
Style: Saltbox
First floor: 1,368 square feet
Second floor: 1,046 square feet
Total: 2,414 square feet
Bedrooms: 4
Bathrooms: 2½
Price schedule: B

The center hall of this Colonial, leading to the dining room, living room, and back to the kitchen, ensures smooth traffic flow to both formal and casual living zones. A wide gable extension adds welcome space upstairs for larger bedrooms and baths.

Two windows in the dining room overlook the front yard of the house.

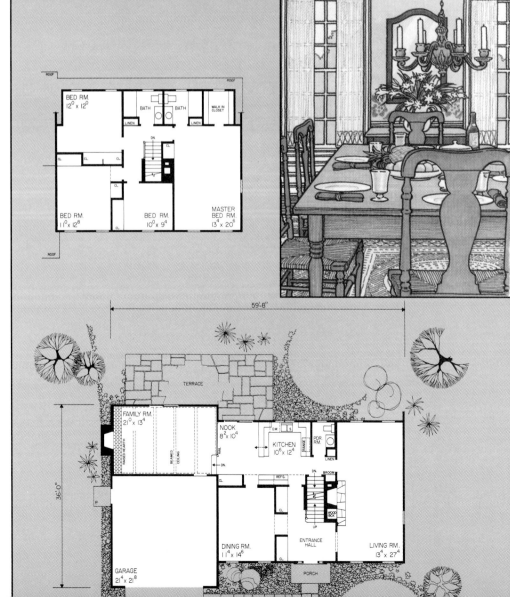

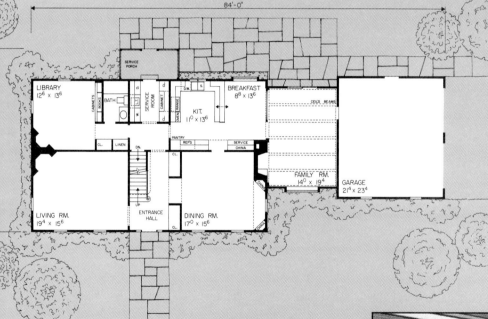

84'-0"

LIBRARY
12⁶ x 13⁶

BATH

SERVICE
ROOM

BREAKFAST
8⁸ x 13⁶

KIT.
11⁰ x 13⁶

CEILG. BEAMS

CABINETS

BOOKS

W.
C

CABINET

OVEN RANGE

D.W.

S

PANTRY

REFG

SERVICE
CHINA

CL.

LINEN

CL.

DN.

LIVING RM.
19⁴ x 15⁶

UP

ENTRANCE
HALL

DINING RM.
17⁰ x 15⁶

FAMILY RM.
14⁰ x 19⁴

GARAGE
21⁴ x 23⁴

PLAN J2157

Type: Two-story
Style: Dutch Colonial
First floor: 1,720 square feet
Second floor: 1,205 square feet
Total: 2,925 square feet
Bedrooms: 3 + library
Bathrooms: 3
Price schedule: C

Dormer windows and a wide rear gable bring extra light and space to the upstairs of this Dutch Colonial. Inside, there is a tremendous amount of livability. The downstairs features a living room and library, both with cozy corner fireplaces. The U-shaped kitchen connects with the dining room and family room.

ROOF

VANITY

CL.

CL.

DRESSING
ROOM

BATH

BATH

BED RM.
14⁸ x 12⁶

LINEN

CL.

CABT
BOOK

DN.

BOOK
CAB'T

BOOK

MASTER
BED RM.
17⁰ x 15⁶

CL.

BED RM.
14⁸ x 11⁴

CL.

CEILG. CLIP

CL.

CEILG. CLIP

CL.

ROOF

ROOF

The family room boasts a beamed ceiling and large fireplace.

PLAN J2697

Type: 1½-story
Style: Dutch Colonial
First floor: 1,764 square feet
Second floor: 1,506 square feet
Total: 3,270 square feet
Bedrooms: 4
Bathrooms: 3½
Price schedule: C

Front and rear covered porches provide ample space for relaxing outdoors. Inside, the floor plan is both gracious and practical. Highlights include fireplaces in the living room, dining room, and family room, a U-shaped kitchen with snack bar and adjacent pantry and laundry room. The spacious second floor houses four bedrooms and three full baths. Notice the master with its dressing room and whirlpool!

One of the four upstairs bedrooms contains an arched window set into the exterior wall.

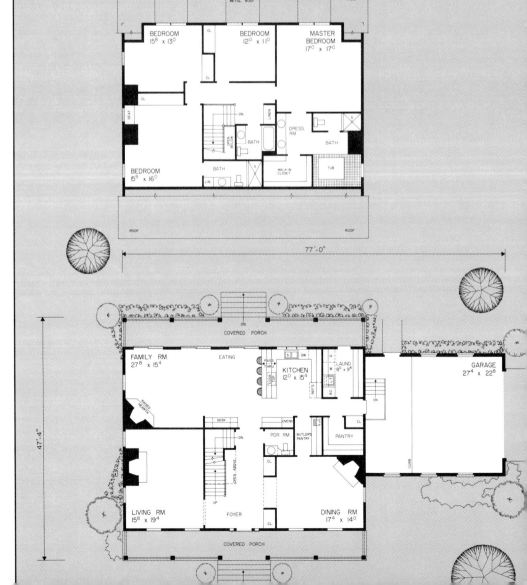

PLAN J2320

Type: Two-story
Style: Dutch Colonial
First floor: 1,856 square feet
Second floor: 1,171 square feet
Total: 3,027 square feet
Bedrooms: 3 or 4 (study)
Bathrooms: 2½
Price schedule: C

This carefully planned design separates formal and informal living areas. The living room and dining room are perfect for entertaining. The large family room provides casual living space. The kitchen features a U-shaped working area, an eating and sitting area, and a fireplace.

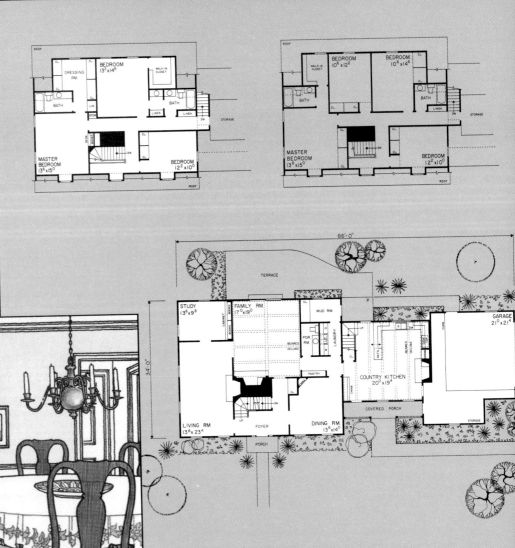

A built-in corner cupboard in the dining room stores and displays china.

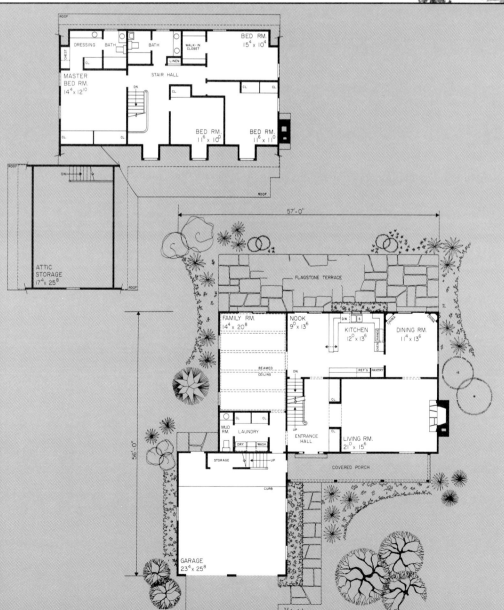

PLAN J2364

Type: Two-story
Style: Dutch Colonial
First floor: 1,440 square feet
Second floor: 1,206 square feet
Total: 2,646 square feet
Bedrooms: 4
Bathrooms: 2½
Price schedule: B

The projecting garage makes this plan ideal for a narrow lot. Inside, this livable design contains many highlights. Note the spaciousness and convenient placement of the rooms. The entrance hall leads to both the living room and back to the kitchen with an eating nook and sliding glass door onto a terrace. The adjacent dining room has built-in china shelves. Upstairs are four bedrooms, several with dormer windows, and two baths. Also note the attic space over the garage. What an attractive, efficiently-planned home!

PLAN J2100

Type: Two-story
Style: Gambrel
First floor: 1,682 square feet
Second floor: 1,344 square feet
Third floor: 780 square feet
Total: 3,806 square feet
Bedrooms: 4
Bathrooms: 2½ + powder room
Price schedule: C

Consider this gambrel-roofed Colonial with charming widow's walk and chimney pots. Bonus space resides on the third floor which can be used for a play room, guest room, or study/studio. Four second-floor bedrooms include a fine master with full bath and dressing area. The first-floor features include a dining room with corner china cabinets, a cozy study, and fireplaces in the family room and living room. A pass-through counter from the breakfast room to the U-shaped kitchen provides a good measure of convenience. Don't miss the abundance of built-ins and the barbecue in the kitchen.

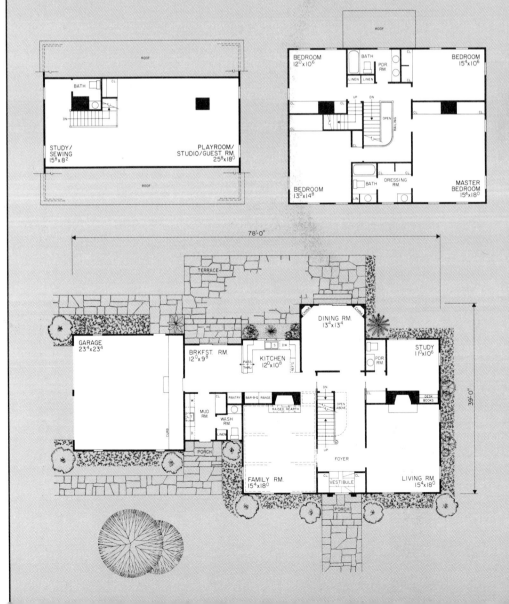

PLAN J2978

Type: Two-story
Style: Gambrel
First floor: 1,451 square feet
Second floor: 1,268 square feet
Third floor: 746 square feet
Total: 3,465 square feet
Bedrooms: 3 + exercise studio
Bathrooms: 3½
Price schedule: C

The Nathaniel Hawthorne house, constructed in Salem, Massachusetts around 1730, was the inspiration for this two-story gambrel. This modern version shows off its interior living space in a family-pleasing country kitchen with island and built-in desk, library, and formal living and dining rooms. The rear garage attaches to the main house via a mud room with adjacent laundry and washroom. The second floor highlight is the luxurious master bedroom with His and Hers closets and a heavenly whirlpool spa. Notice the double vanities. Third floor space leaves room for guests and expansion.

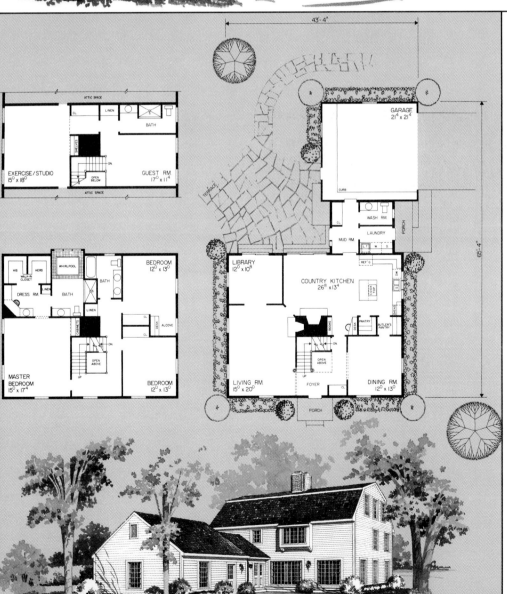

Third floor

ATTIC SPACE
CL
LINEN
BATH
SHELVES
EXERCISE/STUDIO
15⁰ x 18⁰
OPEN BELOW
DN
GUEST RM
17⁰ x 11⁴
ATTIC SPACE

Second floor

HIS
WALK-IN CLOSET
WHIRLPOOL
BEDROOM
12⁰ x 13⁰
HERS
BATH
DRESS. RM
LINEN
BATH
CABINETS
LINEN
CL
CL
DESK
ALCOVE
CL
OPEN ABOVE
UP
MASTER BEDROOM
15⁰ x 17⁴
BEDROOM
12⁰ x 13⁰

First floor

43'-4"

GARAGE
21⁴ x 21⁴
CURB
TERRACE
CL
WASH. RM
PORCH
MUD RM
LAUNDRY
REF G
LIBRARY
12⁰ x 10⁸
COUNTRY KITCHEN
26⁸ x 13⁴
ISLAND
PANTRY
BUTLER'S PANTRY
BOOKS
OPEN ABOVE
UP
LIVING RM.
15⁰ x 20⁰
FOYER
CL
DINING RM.
12⁰ x 13⁰
PORCH

66'-4"

PLAN J1887

Type: Two-story
Style: Gambrel
First floor: 1,518 square feet
Second floor: 1,144 square feet
Total: 2,662 square feet
Bedrooms: 4
Bathrooms: 2½
Price schedule: B

An historical classic, this gambrel offers family living with perfect proportions. Enjoy casual gatherings in the beamed-ceiling family room or accommodate formal occasions in the large living room. Both have fireplaces for warmth. The country kitchen is enhanced with built-ins including an island worktop to save steps. Second-floor sleeping is accomplished in four well-situated bedrooms. Note the double vanity in the master bedroom as well as a walk-in closet here and walk-in linen closet in the hall. An extra-wide terrace runs the width of the house and is accessed by sliding glass doors in the family room.

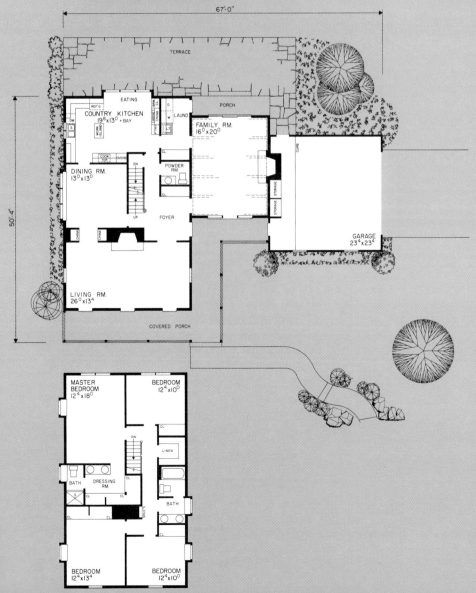

PLAN J2907

Type: Two-story
Style: Gambrel
First floor: 1,546 square feet
Second floor: 1,144 square feet
Total: 2,690 square feet
Bedrooms: 4
Bathrooms: 2½
Price schedule: B

Though its floor plan is nearly identical to Plan J1887 on the previous page, this design has an exterior look that bespeaks farmhouse traditions—rambling covered porches to the front and side and a second porch off the family room to the rear. All of the other amenities are found here including abundant built-in storage, two fireplaces, and plenty of room for formal and informal entertaining. Whichever look you choose, expect gracious livability in a well-planned design.

PLAN J2131

Type: Two-story
Style: Gambrel
First floor: 1,214 square feet
Second floor: 1,097 square feet
Total: 2,311 square feet
Bedrooms: 4
Bathrooms: 2½
Price schedule: B

The embodiment of Early Colonial architecture, this lovely Gambrel features fine detailing and an excellent floor plan. Notice formal and informal areas and accommodating master suite.

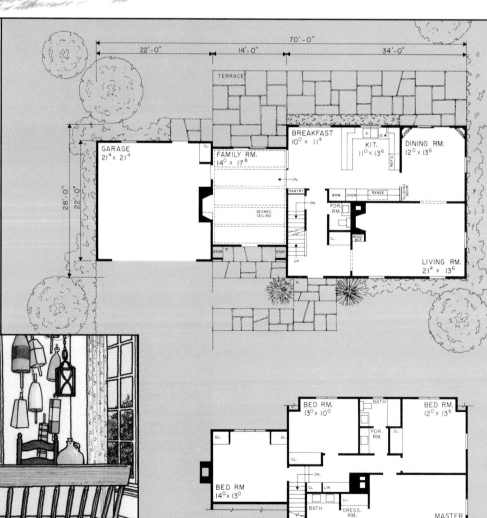

Bench seating lends a touch of tradition to the nook.

PLAN J2531

Type: Two-story
Style: Gambrel
First floor: 1,353 square feet
Second floor: 1,208 square feet
Total: 2,561 square feet
Bedrooms: 3 or 4 (study)
Bathrooms: 2½
Price schedule: B

With roots in New England history, this charmer takes a quantum leap into the 20th Century for its floor plan. Patterned for active living, the plan leads from front entry to spacious formal living and dining rooms to a large kitchen/nook area. The family room is tucked away with rear terrace access through sliding glass doors. In the service entrance is storage space as well as accommodations for a washer and dryer and a freezer. The nearby powder room is a convenient addition. Use all upstairs rooms as sleeping quarters or turn one into a private study to serve the sunken master suite.

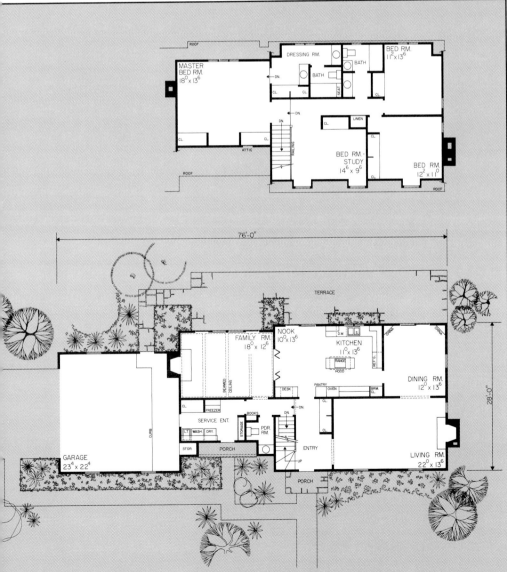

PLAN J2713

Type: 1½-story
Style: Gambrel
First floor: 1,830 square feet
Second floor: 1,056 square feet
Total: 2,886 square feet
Bedrooms: 3 or 4 (study)
Bathrooms: 3
Price schedule: C

A delightful mix of brick and wood beckons an inspection of interior graces. Don't overlook two fireplaces (one with raised hearth) and plentiful use of sliding glass to two rear terraces. A first-floor study doubles as a guest room.

A family room is enhanced with carefully selected interior details.

BED RM.
11⁴x13⁶

BATH

CL.

PDR.
RM.

BED RM.
12⁰x10⁰

CL.

CL.

STUDY-
BED RM.
12⁰x13⁰

DN. | DN.

LINEN

CL.

MASTER
BED RM.
17⁸x12⁰

DRESS
RM.

CL.

BATH

S.

CL.

66'-0"

32'-0" 12'-0" 22'-0"

TERRACE

DINING RM.
11⁴x13⁶

D.W. | S.

REFG.

KITCHEN
10⁸x13⁶

BREAKFAST
9⁰x11⁰

FAMILY RM.
12⁰x17⁴

PANTRY

RANGE

O.

CHINA

DN. CHINA

DN.

RAISED
HEARTH

W.R.

CL.

WOOD
BOX

ENTRY

CL. | SEAT | CL.

UP

GARAGE
21⁴x21⁴

LIVING RM.
21⁴x13⁶

R

PLAN J1777

Type: Two-story
Style: Gambrel
First floor: 1,142 square feet
Second floor: 1,010 square feet
Total: 2,152 square feet
Bedrooms: 3 or 4 (study)
Bathrooms: 2½
Price schedule: B

Authenticity outside, comfortable living inside. That's the
promise of this pretty design.
Separate family and living rooms
keep various activities in their
places — all within range of the
formal dining room and breakfast
nook attached to an efficient
kitchen. The raised-hearth fireplace has its own wood box for
adequate storage of dry firewood.
Rooms on the second floor include a modern master bedroom
and a fourth bedroom that con-
verts easily to a snug study. Closets abound throughout the plan
and there are built-in china cabinets in the nook.

PLAN J2224

Type: Two-story
Style: Gambrel
First floor: 1,567 square feet
Second floor: 1,070 square feet
Total: 2,637 square feet
Bedrooms: 3 + playroom
Bathrooms: 2½
Price schedule: B

Rural New England-style comfort for family living! Notice the extra large living room with fireplace and built-ins. The family kitchen is kept snug with another fireplace and adds charm with an exposed-beam ceiling. Its efficiency is enhanced by the center work island and built-in china buffet. Children have their own space in a playroom with rear terrace access. The master suite on the second floor holds still another fireplace and has a large walk-in closet. Bonus space over the garage can later become a study or maid's or guest's quarters.

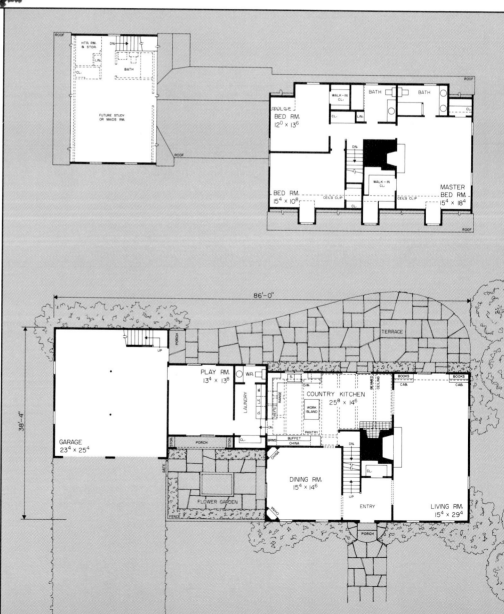

PLAN J2897

Type: Two-story
Style: Gambrel
First floor: 1,648 square feet
Second floor: 1,140 square feet
Total: 2,788 square feet
Bedrooms: 3 + study
Bathrooms: 2½
Price schedule: C

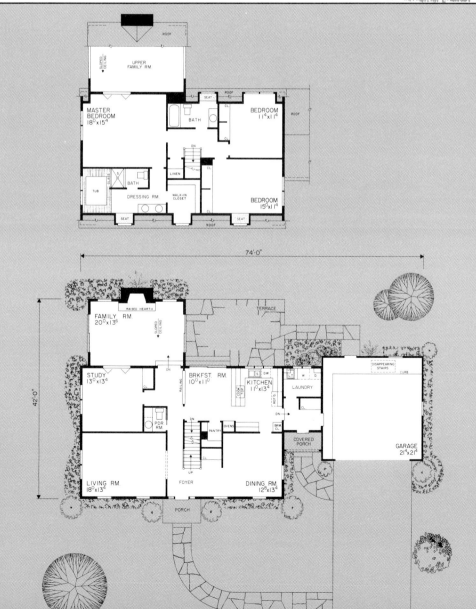

This plan has all the characteristics of thoughtful design. With formal areas to the front and more casual areas to the rear, livability is maximized. A sunken, two-story family room features sloped ceiling and raised-hearth fireplace. Close by is the more private study with its own closet. A pampering master bath accents the master suite on the second floor. Look for twin vanities, large walk-in closet, and separate tub and shower. Two more bedrooms share a full bath of their own. Window seats adorn the dormers on this floor.

PLAN J2680

Type: Two-story
Style: Dutch Colonial
First floor: 1,707 square feet
Second floor: 1,439 square feet
Total: 3,146 square feet
Bedrooms: 4
Bathrooms: 3½ + powder room
Price schedule: C

With its gambrel roof and twin chimney stacks, this home retains all the charm of its Early American heritage. Past the covered front porch lies a marvelous interior plan as well. From the beamed-ceiling country kitchen to corner firepaces in the living room and study, this plan is perfect. Take note of covered porches flanking the formal dining room and second floor with four bedrooms and three full baths. The sunken bedroom over the garage would make a perfect guest room or could be used as a nursery for infants.

A country kitchen with stone hearth is a convivial gathering spot for family.

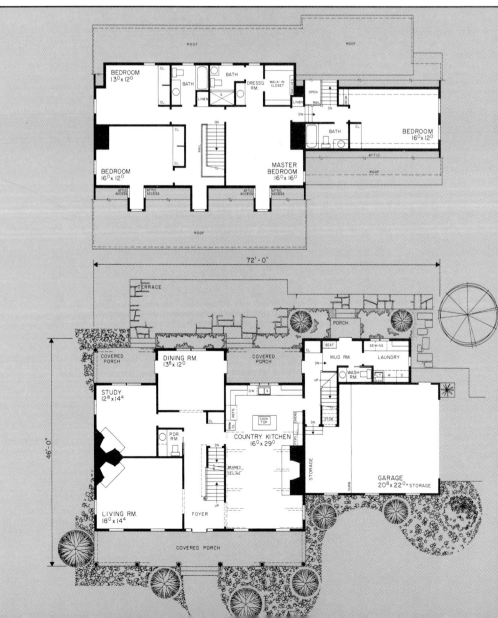

PLAN J2189

Type: Two-story
Style: Gambrel
First floor: 1,134 square feet
Second floor: 1,063 square feet
Total: 2,197 square feet
Bedrooms: 3
Bathrooms: 2½
Price schedule: B

Beyond a wonderfully symmetrical exterior, this Colonial offers all the amenities to satisfy today's living patterns. A quiet study with built-ins opposes the formal living room. To the rear are formal dining room (with large bay window), kitchen, and country-style family room with fireplace and woodbox. Upstairs, a master bedroom suite is joined by two more bedrooms and a full bath. Convenient and practical, an area above the garage allows easy access and ample room for storage.

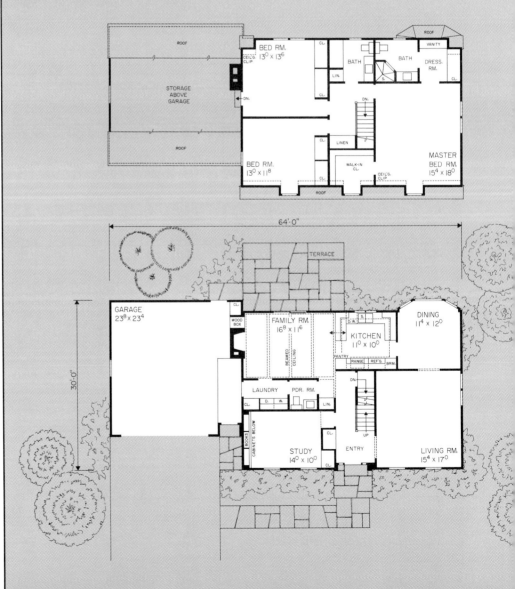

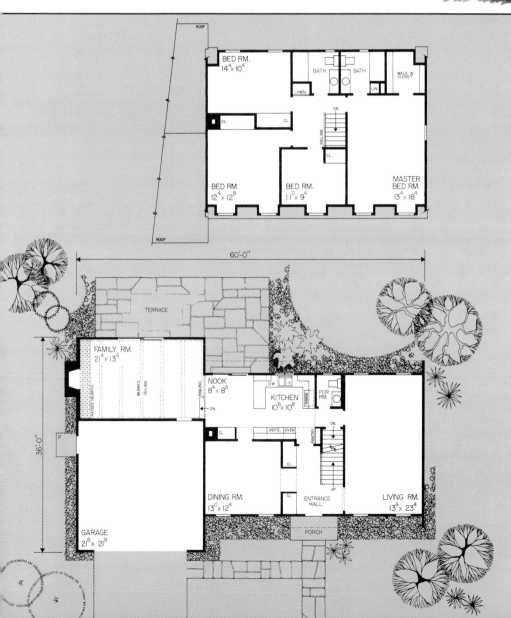

PLAN J2617

Type: Two-story
Style: Gambrel
First floor: 1,223 square feet
Second floor: 1,018 square feet
Total: 2,241 square feet
Bedrooms: 4
Bathrooms: 2½
Price schedule: B

A gambrel roof line and dormer windows signal Colonial style at its finest. Inside, look for a well-planned design with large living room and family room at opposite ends of the house. The convenient kitchen has an attached nook and is just across the hall from a formal dining room. A large walk-in closet enhances the master suite on the second floor, with three more bedrooms sharing a full bath. A large two-car garage connects directly to the house via the family room and also has an outside entrance with small porch.

PLAN J2650

Type: Two-story
Style: Gambrel
First floor: 1,451 square feet
Second floor: 1,091 square feet
Total: 2,542 square feet
Bedrooms: 3
Bathrooms: 2½
Price schedule: B

From covered porch to rear terrace, this plan has it all. Be sure to notice the large gathering room, cozy study, and built-in amenities throughout.

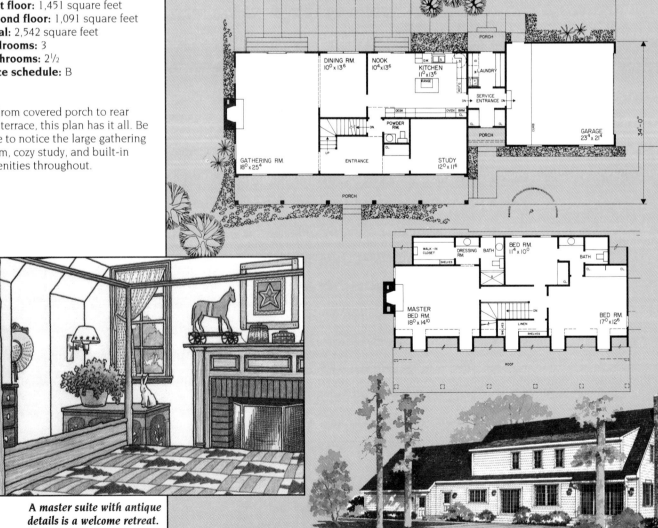

A master suite with antique details is a welcome retreat.

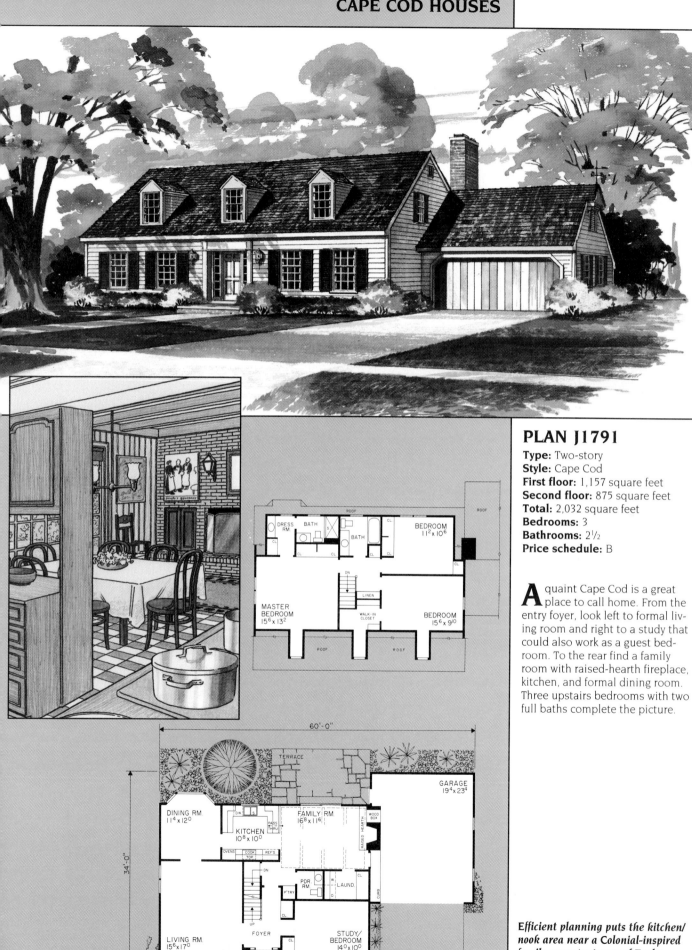

PLAN J1791

Type: Two-story
Style: Cape Cod
First floor: 1,157 square feet
Second floor: 875 square feet
Total: 2,032 square feet
Bedrooms: 3
Bathrooms: 2½
Price schedule: B

A quaint Cape Cod is a great place to call home. From the entry foyer, look left to formal living room and right to a study that could also work as a guest bedroom. To the rear find a family room with raised-hearth fireplace, kitchen, and formal dining room. Three upstairs bedrooms with two full baths complete the picture.

Efficient planning puts the kitchen/nook area near a Colonial-inspired family room (note use of Early American accents).

PLAN J2699

Type: 1½-story
Style: Cape Cod
First floor: 2,188 square feet
Second floor: 858 square feet
Total: 3,046 square feet
Bedrooms: 3
Bathrooms: 3½ + powder room
Price schedule: C

This gorgeous Cape Cod is filled with surprises. Its New England-based facade gives no hint of the modern floor planning inside. From an amenity-filled master suite to a giant-sized country kitchen, there's room for the entire family. Entertain in the two-story living room and adjacent dining room. Pursue favorite TV or music activities in the media room. Children's rooms and a lounge on the second floor assure total privacy away from the master suite. It is well-appointed with a lounge, whirlpool spa, and gigantic walk-in closet.

Double-height fan lights add drama and a wealth of natural sunlight.

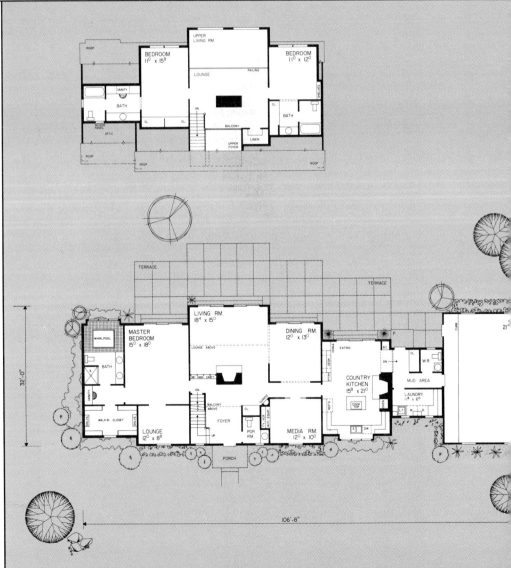

PLAN J2657

Type: Two-story
Style: Cape Cod
First floor: 1,217 square feet
Second floor: 868 square feet
Total: 2,085 square feet
Bedrooms: 3
Bathrooms: 2½
Price schedule: B

Traditional Cape Cod character highlights this home's exterior: clapboard siding, small-paned windows, and a transom-lit entrance with flanking carriage lamps. Take time to appreciate the thoughtful interior plan.

This country kitchen owes much to wood and brick accents.

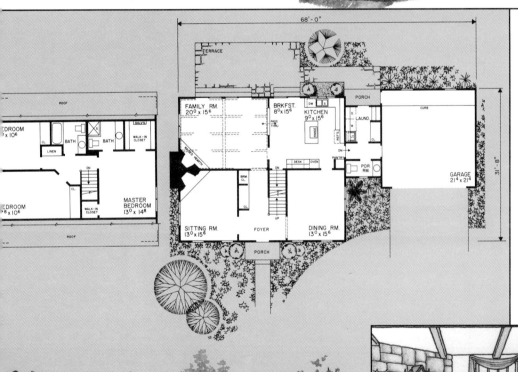

PLAN J2644

Type: 1½-story
Style: Cape Cod
First floor: 1,349 square feet
Second floor: 836 square feet
Total: 2,185 square feet
Bedrooms: 3
Bathrooms: 2½
Price schedule: B

A delightful 1½-story houses many fine features within its framework. Special highlights include corner fireplaces in sitting and family rooms, an island range in the kitchen, and generous storage throughout.

A generously sized family room is more cozy with a corner fireplace.

PLAN J2655

Type: 1½-story
Style: Cape Cod
First floor: 893 square feet
Second floor: 652 square feet
Total: 1,545 square feet
Bedrooms: 2
Bathrooms: 2½
Price schedule: A

This is a plan that's small in size yet long on good looks and livability. Its appealing exterior lines and second-story dormers lead the way to a convenient plan with front study, living room, dining room, and a kitchen with nook. A nearby service area includes a laundry and washroom. Two bedrooms and two full baths are located on the second floor. Be sure to note the rear screened porch.

A place to gather and converse, the Early American living room speaks of warmth and grace.

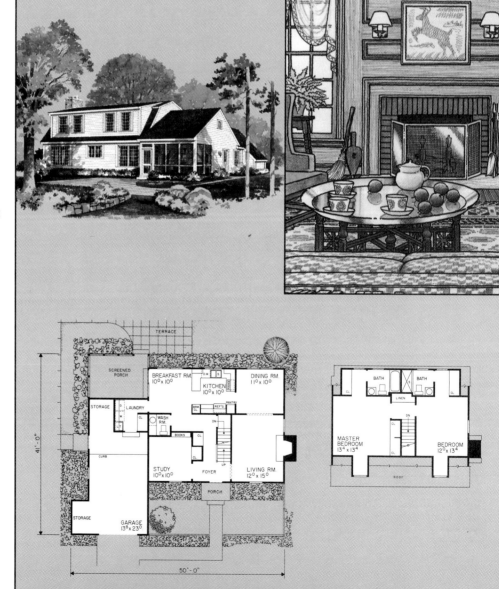

PLAN J2656

Type: 1½-story
Style: Cape Cod
First floor: 1,122 square feet
Second floor: 884 square feet
Total: 2,006 square feet
Bedrooms: 3
Bathrooms: 2½
Price schedule: B

Relying on Cape Cod cottages of the 18th Century for its floor plan, this home provides a marvelous use of space. The master bedroom offers amenities well beyond what might be expected.

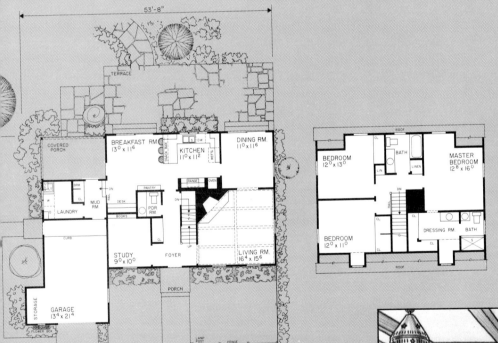

Beamed ceilings lend an air of authenticity to this living room.

69

BEDROOM
12¹⁰ x 9⁸

BEDROOM
12¹⁰ x 9⁸

DN

LINEN

BATH

BATH

MASTER
BEDROOM
11¹⁰ x 14⁰

ROOF

ROOF

32'-0"

TERRACE

30'-0"

DINING RM.
10⁸ x 12⁰

COUNTRY KITCHEN
20⁰ x 13⁰ 15⁸

REFG

RANGE

DN

PDR
RM

BRM
CL

PTRY

UP

FOYER

BOOKS

LIVING RM.
20⁰ x 13⁰

PORCH

PLAN J2682

Type: 1½-story
Style: Cape Cod
First floor: 976 square feet
(basic plan)
1,230 square feet
(expanded plan)
Second floor: 744 square feet
(both plans)
Total: 1,720 square feet
(basic plan)
1,970 square feet
(expanded plan)
Bedrooms: 3
Bathrooms: 2½
Price schedule: A

This expandable Cape is perfect for growing families. The basic plan features a large living room, a dining room with a bay window, a spacious country kitchen with a fireplace, and three bedrooms upstairs. The expanded version offers downstairs study and covered porch and attic storage or future room on the second floor.

A brick fireplace adorns this ample country kitchen.

PLAN J2635

Type: 1½-story
Style: Cape Cod
First floor: 1,317 square feet,
Second floor: 681 square feet
Total: 1,998 square feet
Bedrooms: 3
Bathrooms: 1½
Price schedule: A

The shingled exterior of this 1½-story cottage is reminiscent of Nantucket Island. This updated version of a style popular in the 18th-century benefits from a modern floor plan. A U-shaped kitchen adjoins the beamed-ceilinged keeping room. This room and the adjacent living room form a spacious living area. Like most Capes, this home features a first-floor bedroom which could double as a study.

The beamed-ceilinged keeping room is located at the back of the house, beneath the low, lean-to roof.

PLAN J2636

Type: 1½-story
Style: Cape Cod
First floor: 1,121 square feet
Second floor: 747 square feet
Total: 1,868 square feet
Bedrooms: 3
Bathrooms: 2
Price schedule: A

Here's another 1½-story home—a type of house favored by many of Cape Cod's early whalers. As with most Capes, there is a downstairs bedroom. The dining room and living room include built-in shelves and cabinets and the kitchen has an eating area. Upstairs are two more bedrooms, a compartmented bath, and loads of closet space. Compact and economical, this is an excellent house to finish off in stages.

The sloped ceiling beneath the roofline of the master bedroom creates the cozy feeling.

PLAN J1970

Type: Two-story
Style: Cape Cod
First floor: 1,664 square feet,
Second floor: 1,116 square feet
Total: 2,780 square feet
Bedrooms: 3 + library
Bathrooms: 2½
Price schedule: C

This classic Cape Cod design includes two entrances—a formal entrance for guests and a secondary entrance leading to the family room. Inside is a spacious floor plan which includes large living and family rooms, an ample kitchen, and a library with built-in bookshelves. Three bedrooms and two baths upstairs complete the plan.

A country kitchen, outfitted with a barbecue range, lies at the end of the generous entry hall.

PLAN J2396

Type: Two-story
Style: Cape Cod
First floor: 1,616 square feet
Second floor: 993 square feet
Total: 2,609 square feet
Bedrooms: 4
Bathrooms: 3
Price schedule: B

This home features another picturesque facade from the pages of our Colonial heritage. This updated version contains a large family room with beamed ceiling and a convenient U-shaped kitchen with a pass-through to the breakfast nook. The downstairs bedroom may serve as a study.

A fireplace dominates the interior wall of the living room.

PLAN J2145

Type: 1½-story
Style: Cape Cod
First floor: 1,182 square feet
Second floor: 708 square feet
Total: 1,890 square feet
Bedrooms: 4
Bathrooms: 2
Price schedule: A

Particularly suited to a narrow lot, this Cape is a mere 44 feet wide. The covered porch behind the house adds living space and, with the garage, snugly encloses a flower court. Two bedrooms upstairs and two down provide peace and quiet.

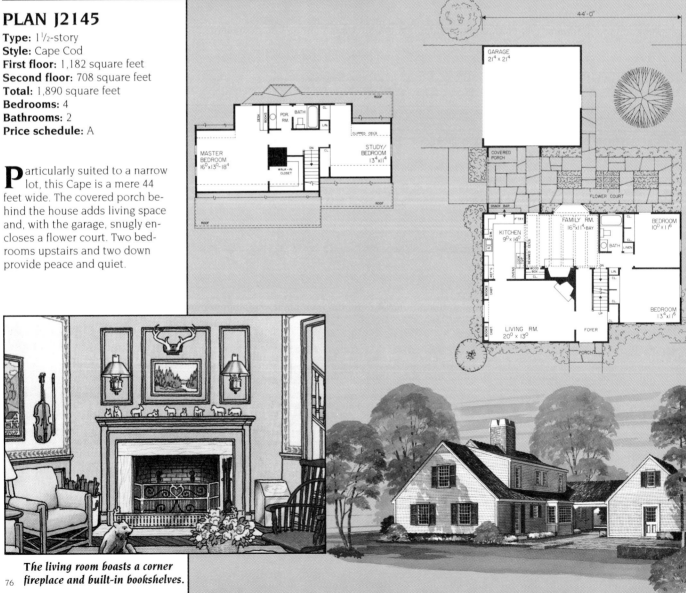

The living room boasts a corner fireplace and built-in bookshelves.

PLAN J2658

Type: 1½-story
Style: Cape Cod
First floor: 1,218 square feet
Second floor: 764 square feet
Total: 1,982 square feet
Bedrooms: 3 + study
Bathrooms: 2½
Price schedule: A

Traditional charm merges with interior livability in this efficient 1½-story home. The living room connects with the formal dining room, which is adjacent to the spacious kitchen. The kitchen features a snack bar and breakfast room, and access to the rear terrace. Next door is a laundry room. A quiet study with a bay window rounds out the first floor. Three upstairs bedrooms include a master with a dressing room. Notice the storage area in the garage.

China cabinets flank the entry connecting the living room to the dining room.

PLAN J2563

Type: 1½-story
Style: Cape Cod
First floor: 1,500 square feet
Second floor: 690 square feet
Total: 2,190 square feet
Bedrooms: 3 + study
Bathrooms: 2
Price schedule: B

This trim Cape has a study, master bedroom, and dining wing that gradually step down in depth and height from the center section of the house. To the rear is an enormous farm kitchen. Upstairs are two bedrooms and a sitting room.

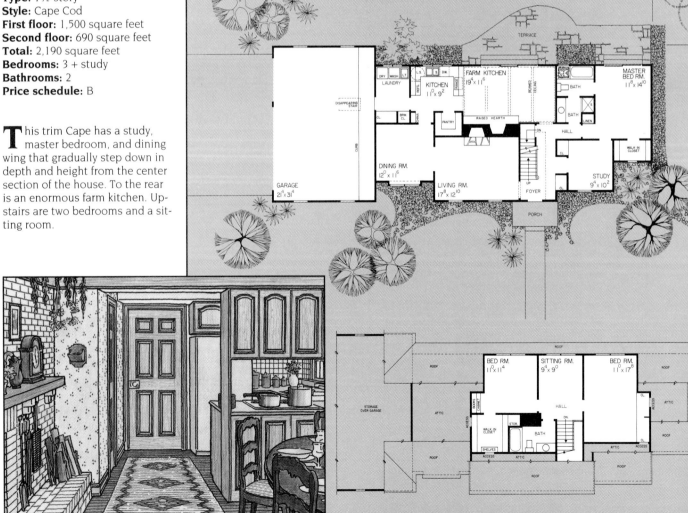

A spacious farm kitchen also serves as a family room.

PLAN J2395

Type: 1½-story
Style: Cape Cod
First floor: 1,481 square feet
Second floor: 861 square feet
Total: 2,342 square feet
Bedrooms: 4
Bathrooms: 3½
Price schedule: B

Three wings augment the space in this snug Cape, one incorporating two downstairs bedrooms, the others enclosing a porch with laundry behind, and a garage. The family and living rooms each contain a fireplace. Two bedrooms upstairs and two down assure utmost privacy.

A spacious beamed family room overlooks the terrace and garden.

PLAN J2689

Type: 1½-story
Style: Cape Cod
First floor: 1,385 square feet
Second floor: 982 square feet
Total: 2,367 square feet
Bedrooms: 3
Bathrooms: 2½
Price schedule: B

The large foyer of this shingled Cape leads to the living room and dining room and to the country kitchen in the rear. This spacious room features an island with a snack bar and a bay window overlooking the back yard. A mud room and laundry room connect the kitchen and garage. In warm weather, the screened porch provides a breezy retreat. Upstairs are three bedrooms and two full baths.

Double glass doors separate the spacious country kitchen from the screened porch.

PLAN J2661

Type: 1½-story
Style: Cape Cod
First floor: 1,020 square feet
Second floor: 777 square feet
Total: 1,797 square feet
Bedrooms: 3 + study
Bathrooms: 2½
Price schedule: A

Ideal for a small lot, this cozy Cape has an amply proportioned interior. The floor plan includes a living room with a corner fireplace, downstairs study, and a spacious country kitchen. Upstairs are three bedrooms and two full baths.

A corner fireplace in the country kitchen faces a bay window.

PLAN J2615

Type: 1½-story
Style: Cape Cod
First floor: 2,563 square feet
Second floor: 552 square feet
Total: 3,115 square feet
Bedrooms: 3 + study
Bathrooms: 2½
Price schedule: D

This grandly amplified Cape features 18th-Century styling coupled with a 20th-Century floor plan. The gracious foyer leads to the large living room, a cozy study, and back to the dining room and kitchen. Perfect for informal entertaining and relaxing, the enormous family room adjoins the kitchen and has a large wet bar and fireplace. The luxurious master suite features twin walk-in closets and opens to a covered porch and cheery solarium with skylights. The second floor includes two spacious bedrooms which share a bath.

The solarium is a unique feature in this spacious Cape.

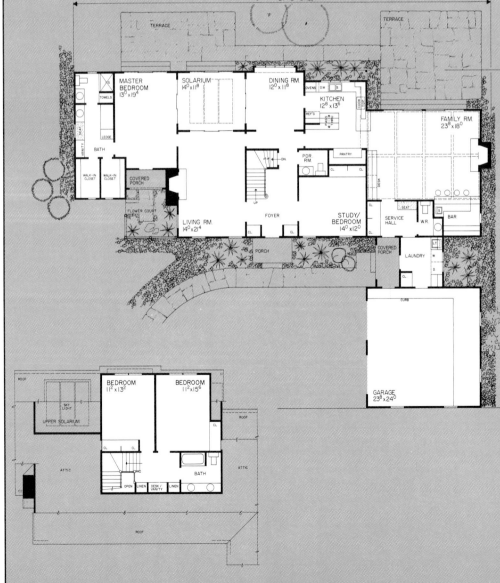

PLAN J1987

Type: 1½-story
Style: Cape Cod
First floor: 1,632 square feet
Second floor: 980 square feet
Total: 2,612 square feet
Bedrooms: 3 or 4 (study)
Bathrooms: 3½
Price schedule: B

This Colonial adaptation offers considerable high-lights: two fireplaces, optional three or four bedrooms, three and a half baths. A flagstone terrace will be enjoyed by all.

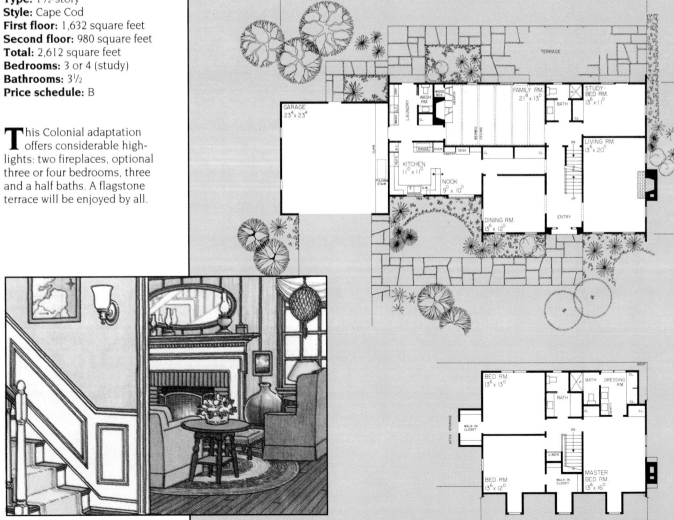

The front entry (with living room beyond) is lighted by a wall sconce.

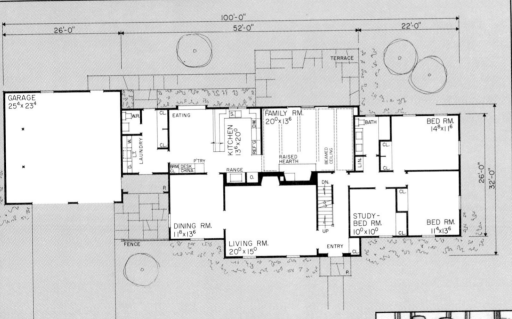

PLAN J1718

Type: 1½-story
Style: Cape Cod
First floor: 2,012 square feet
Second floor: 589 square feet
Total: 2,601 square feet
Bedrooms: 3 or 4 (study)
Bathrooms: 2½
Price schedule: B

A truly special floor plan! The master suite is spacious and private. Living areas easily accommodate a wide variety of activities. The front study could double nicely as a fourth bedroom.

A finely furnished formal living area is essential to traditional design.

PLAN J1901

Type: 1½-story
Style: Cape Cod
First floor: 1,200 square feet
Second floor: 744 square feet
Total: 1,944 square feet
Bedrooms: 2
Bathrooms: 1½
Price schedule: A

Small but eminently livable, this design offers all the options of a much larger plan: formal and informal gathering areas, kitchen with pass-through to nook, study or guest bedroom, fireplace with wood box. Both upstairs bedrooms have their own dressing areas; the master bedroom sports a walk-in closet. Its bath has a double vanity and a linen closet in the hall stores towels and other necessities.

A classically configured formal dining area serves dinner guests beautifully.

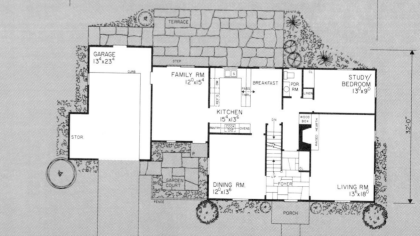

PLAN J2569

Type: 1½-story
Style: Cape Cod
First floor: 1,102 square feet
Second floor: 764 square feet
Total: 1,866 square feet
Bedrooms: 3
Bathrooms: 2½
Price schedule: A

An enchanting Cape version with an open casual living space to the rear. Sliding glass doors in the family and dining rooms and a large bay window in the nook allow an appreciation of indoor-outdoor living. Two terraces add to the enjoyment. Three bedrooms and two full baths are found upstairs. Notice the wealth of closet and storage space that is available on both plans.

A balcony overlook from the second floor of this Cape focuses on the two-story entry.

87

PLAN J2571

Type: 1½-story
Style: Cape Cod
First floor: 1,137 square feet
Second floor: 795 square feet
Total: 1,932 square feet
Bedrooms: 3 or 4 (study)
Bathrooms: 3
Price schedule: A

This attractive Cape Cod overflows with cost-efficiency, from the spacious living room with full-length paned windows to the formal dining room with its classic bay window. Add the well-appointed family room and kitchen plus a bonus study (or optional fourth bedroom) and its true livability is realized. Upstairs are three bedrooms and two baths. The master bedroom features three closets.

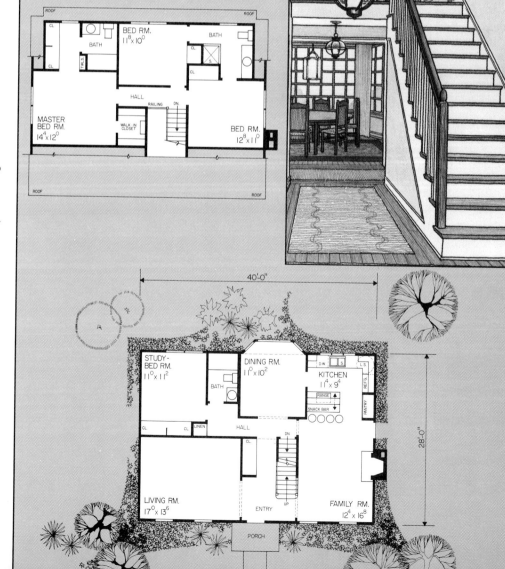

A center hall entry leads back to formal dining or upstairs to three bedrooms and two baths.

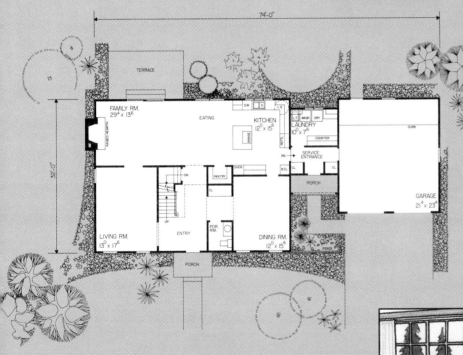

PLAN J2596

Type: 1½-story
Style: Cape Cod
First floor: 1,489 square feet
Second floor: 982 square feet
Total: 2,471 square feet
Bedrooms: 3
Bathrooms: 2½
Price schedule: B

Perfect details from weather vane to covered side entry grace this Cape's facade. And inside there's plenty of living space. Note the fine master suite, with dressing area and walk-in closet, and the handy service area just off the garage.

An open family room gives a feeling of spaciousness to this plan.

PLAN J2162

Type: 1½-story
Style: Cape Cod
First floor: 741 square feet
Second floor: 504 square feet
Total: 1,245 square feet
Bedrooms: 2
Bathrooms: 1½
Price schedule: A

A plan for empty-nesters or small families. Though economically devised, the design uses space wisely and takes advantage of efficient traffic patterns. A study, opposite the living room, might double as a guest bedroom if needed. Notice the walk-in closets in both upstairs bedrooms. Quaint added touches include a cozy fireplace, large rear terrace, and second-story dormer windows.

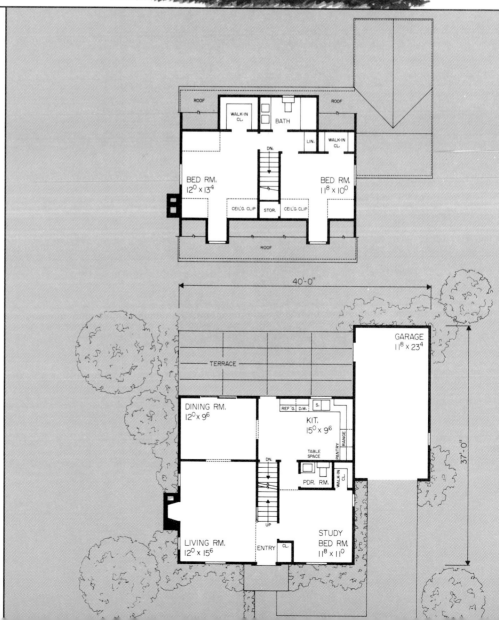

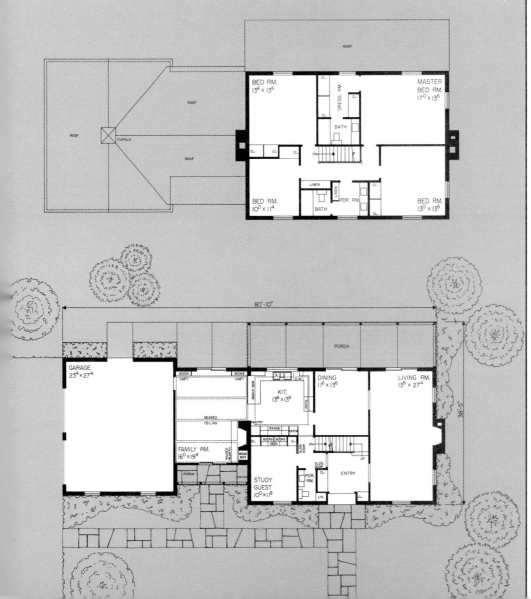

PLAN J2176

Type: Two-story
Style: Georgian
First floor: 1,485 square feet
Second floor: 1,175 square feet
Total: 2,660 square feet
Bedrooms: 4
Bathrooms: 2½
Price schedule: B

Focusing on lifestyles, this plan has a big living room with fireplace at one end and an ample family room at the other end with another fireplace. The efficient kitchen separates the family room from formal dining room. The front study, with built-ins, could be used to serve overnight guests. Upstairs bedrooms include a master bedroom with private bath. Three other bedrooms share a full bath and are served by plenty of linen storage. Notice the large rear porch.

PLAN J2687

Type: Two-story
Style: Georgian
First floor: 1,819 square feet
Second floor: 1,472 square feet
Total: 3,291 square feet
Bedrooms: 4
Bathrooms: 2½
Price schedule: C

Historical exterior styling gives way to a wonderfully up-to-date floor plan. This design has all the amenities that top everyone's wish list: whirlpool spa, country kitchen, two fireplaces, and a greenhouse.

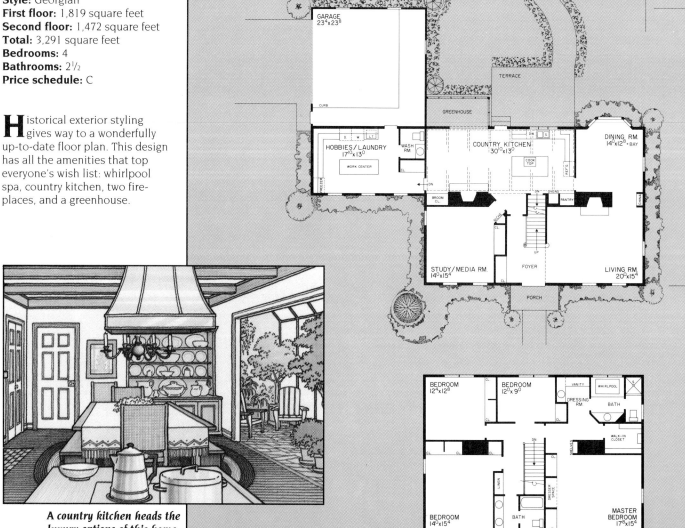

A country kitchen heads the luxury options of this home.

PLAN J2640

Type: Two-story
Style: New England Federal
First floor: 1,386 square feet
Second floor: 1,232 square feet
Total: 2,618 square feet
Bedrooms: 4
Bathrooms: 2½ + powder room
Price schedule: B

Symmetry is the order of the day in this lovely adaptation. Don't miss the many extra features: built-ins, snack bar pass-through between kitchen and family room, rustic beamed ceiling, and attic.

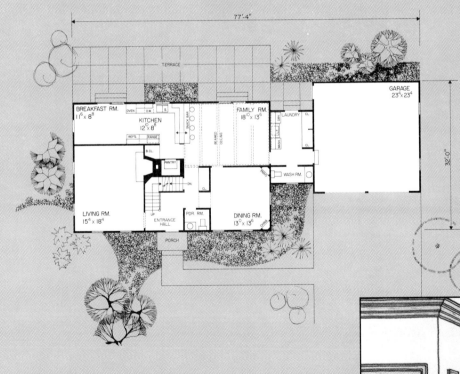

A quaint fan light heralds a standard of traditional styling.

PLAN J2665

Type: Two-story
Style: Georgian
First floor: 1,152 square feet (excludes guest suite and galleries)
Second floor: 1,152 square feet
Total: 2,304 square feet
Bedrooms: 4 + guest suite
Bathrooms: 3½
Price schedule: D

Inspired by George Washington's Mount Vernon, this home makes a grand presentation. The main part of the house is flanked by galleries which connect to matching wings. Inside, the large foyer leads into the living room, keeping room (both with fireplaces), and dining room. Four sets of French doors add an elegant touch and open onto the rear portico. An option to the first-floor guest suite includes a games room with fireplace and spiral staircase. The second-floor option is a loft overlooking the games room below. Four bedrooms on the second floor include a master suite with dressing room, window seat, and fireplace.

Floor-to-ceiling windows flood the galleries with natural light.

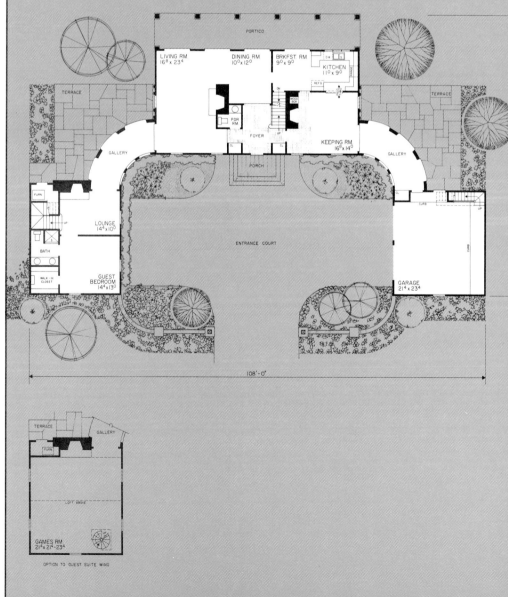

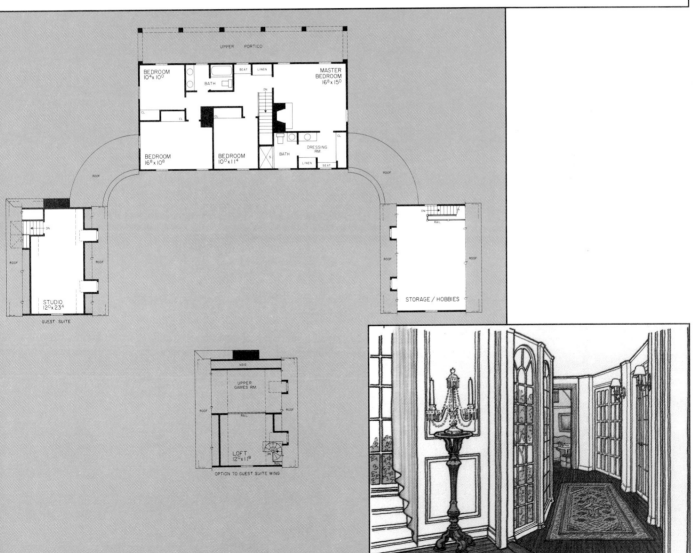

UPPER PORTICO

BEDROOM
10⁴ x 10⁰

SEAT   LINEN

BATH

MASTER
BEDROOM
16⁸ x 15⁰

CL

CL

DN

DRESSING
RM

CL

BEDROOM
16⁸ x 10⁸

BEDROOM
10⁰ x 11⁴

BATH

LINEN

SEAT

ROOF

ROOF

ROOF

DN

ROOF

ROOF

STUDIO
12⁰ x 23⁴

GUEST SUITE

ON

RAIL

STORAGE / HOBBIES

ROOF

ROOF

VOID

UPPER
GAMES RM.

ROOF

ROOF

RAIL

LOFT
12⁰ x 11⁹

DN

OPTION TO GUEST SUITE WING

PLAN J2639

Type: Two-story
Style: Georgian
First floor: 1,556 square feet
Second floor: 1,428 square feet
Total: 2,984 square feet
Bedrooms: 4 + lounge
Bathrooms: 2½
Price schedule: C

The elegant facade of this New England Georgian adaptation boasts a pedimented doorway which gives way to a second-story Palladian window, capped in turn by a pediment projecting from the hipped roof. Interior highlights include fireplaces in the living, dining, and family rooms, a spacious U-shaped kitchen, and an upstairs lounge. Loads of built-ins in the family room, dining room, and kitchen provide plenty of space for convenient storage and display of family treasures.

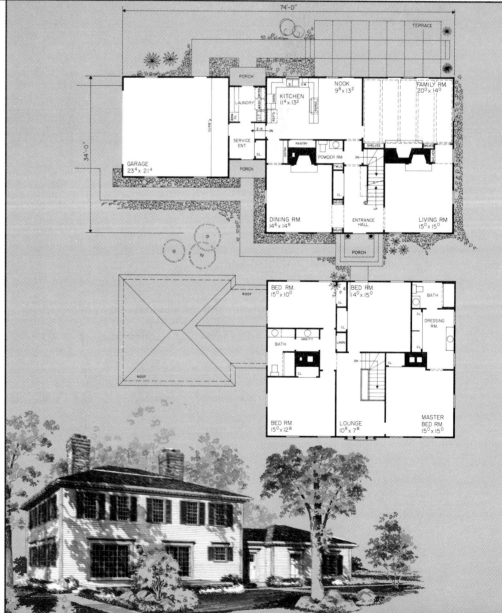

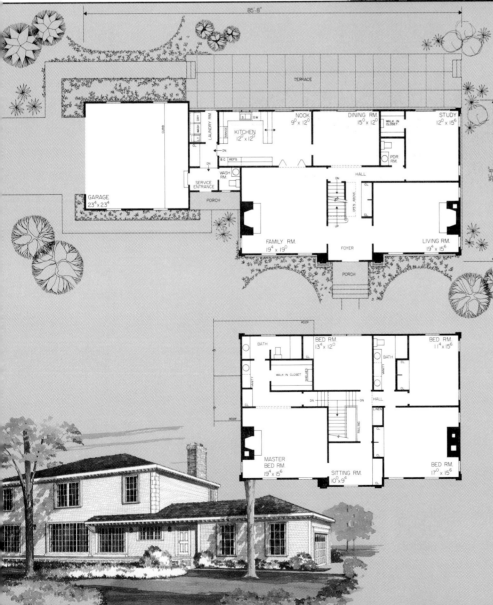

PLAN J2522

Type: Two-story
Style: Georgian
First floor: 1,835 square feet
Second floor: 1,625 square feet
Total: 3,460 square feet
Bedrooms: 4 + study
Bathrooms: 2½ + powder room
Price schedule: C

This wood-frame Georgian adaptation revives the architecture of an earlier period in New England. Its formal facade houses an abundance of spacious livability. The interior features large living and family rooms, each with a fireplace, and a downstairs study. Notice the proximity of the kitchen to the dining room and family room — a nice arrangement for both formal and informal entertaining. The spacious second-floor master suite includes a fireplace, large walk-in closet, and a private sitting room.

97

PLAN J2641

Type: Two-story
Style: Georgian
First floor: 1,672 square feet
Second floor: 1,248 square feet
Total: 2,920 square feet
Bedrooms: 3 or 4 (study)
Bathrooms: 2½
Price schedule: C

This Georgian adaptation from the early 18th Century has plenty of historical background with its classical detailing. The plan promises up-to-date livability with its spacious living room and dining room, U-shaped kitchen, and adjoining family room. The size of your lot need not be large, either; careful placement of the family room and garage to the rear make this plan ideal for a narrow lot. Don't miss the corner fireplace, flagstone terrace, beamed-ceiling family room, and large bedrooms.

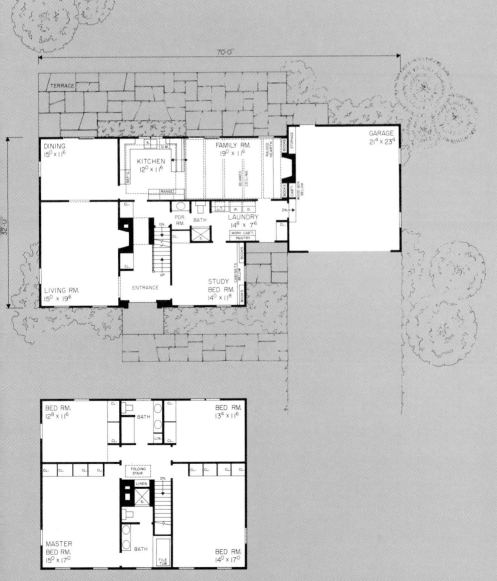

PLAN J2188

Type: Two-story
Style: Georgian
First floor: 1,440 square feet
Second floor: 1,280 square feet
Total: 2,720 square feet
Bedrooms: 4 + study
Bathrooms: 3
Price schedule: C

Along with exterior charm, this Early American design has outstanding livability to offer its occupants. The formal areas of the living room and dining room are located to the left of the entry. The adjoining kitchen and family room occupy the rear and have access to a spacious terrace. Also downstairs is a corner study which may serve as a bedroom. Four more bedrooms are on the second floor. Built-ins abound in the family room and laundry and two downstairs fireplaces add a warm glow.

99

PLAN J2600

Type: Two-story
Style: Georgian
First floor: 1,408 square feet
Second floor: 1,408 square feet
Total: 2,816 square feet
Bedrooms: 4
Bathrooms: 2½
Price schedule: C

The gambrel roof of this home accommodates an optional third floor. The entrance hall, punctuated by a graceful staircase, opens into the living room and the beamed family room. The dining room has corner china cabinets; the kitchen, a spacious breakfast room.

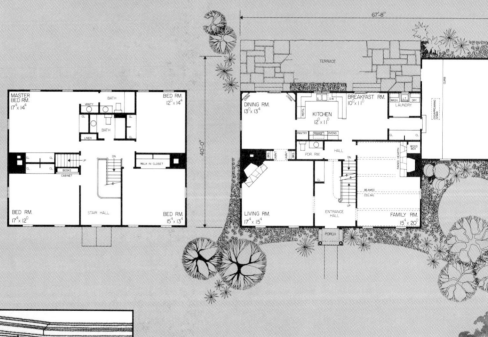

The living room has a corner fireplace.

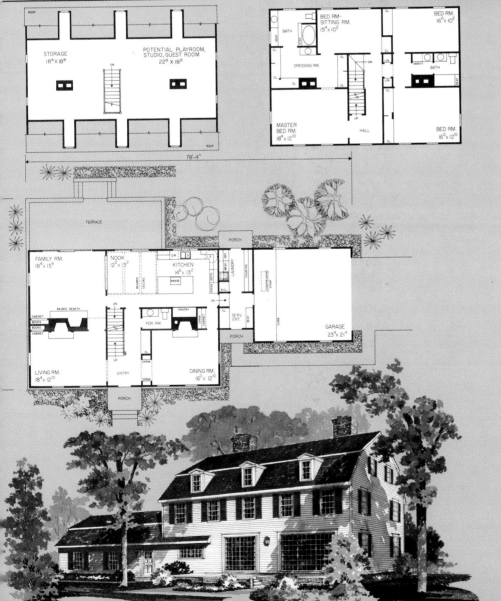

PLAN J2556

Type: Three-story
Style: Georgian
First floor: 1,675 square feet
Second floor: 1,472 square feet
Total: 3,147 square feet
Bedrooms: 3 + optional studio/guest room
Bathrooms: 2½
Price schedule: C

This gambrel-roofed home features plenty of living space. The entry hall leads into the living room and dining room, each with a fireplace. Connecting to the living room is the family room which is open to the L-shaped kitchen and eating nook. Sliding glass doors in the family room and kitchen provide great views of the backyard and access to the rear terrace. Upstairs are three bedrooms and a sitting room. The third floor contains storage space and a bonus room, to be completed later.

PLAN J2301

Type: Two-story
Style: Georgian
First floor: 2,044 square feet
Second floor: 1,815 square feet
Total: 3,859 square feet
Bedrooms: 4 + sitting room
Bathrooms: 3½ + powder room
Price schedule: D

Reminiscent of architecture in the deep South, this finely detailed home is exquisite, indeed. The facade of this home features a pedimented doorway with a double set of steps and a pediment projection on the roof. Study the contemporary floor plan and the living patterns it offers. The living room and family room each boast large fireplaces; the dining room also has a fireplace. The kitchen includes a snack bar and an adjacent tea room with a sliding glass door onto the terrace. Upstairs are four bedrooms and a sitting room.

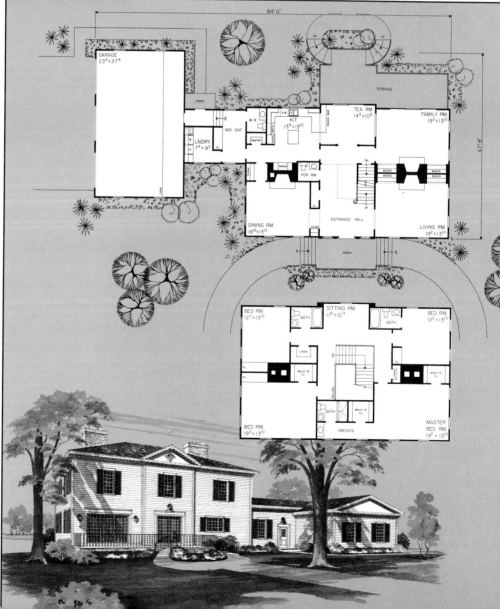

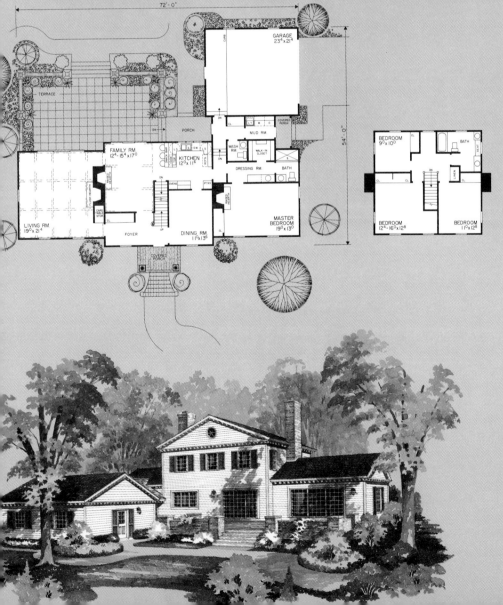

PLAN J2667

Type: Two-story
Style: Georgian
First floor: 1,827 square feet
Second floor: 697 square feet
Total: 2,524 square feet
Bedrooms: 4
Bathrooms: 2½
Price schedule: B

Two one-story wings flank the two-story center section of this Georgian design. The left wing is a huge living room; the right, the master bedroom suite, service area and garage. The kitchen, dining room, and family room are centrally located with three bedrooms above. Notice the large, raised terrace to the rear with access from the living room and family room. Study this plan and imagine your family occupying this carefully zoned home.

PLAN J2221

Type: Two-story
Style: Georgian
First floor: 1,726 square feet
Second floor: 1,440 square feet
Total: 3,166 square feet
Bedrooms: 3 + library
Bathrooms: 3
Price schedule: C

A Georgian Colonial adaptation on a grand scale. The authentic front entrance is delightfully detailed. Two massive end chimneys that service four fireplaces are in keeping with architecture of its day. Inside, both the living room and the library have corner fireplaces; an adjacent full bath makes the library a potential guest room. Also downstairs are a U-shaped kitchen, a large dining room, and a beamed family room with a fireplace. Upstairs are three good-sized bedrooms and two full baths. There's plenty of storage space in the attic.

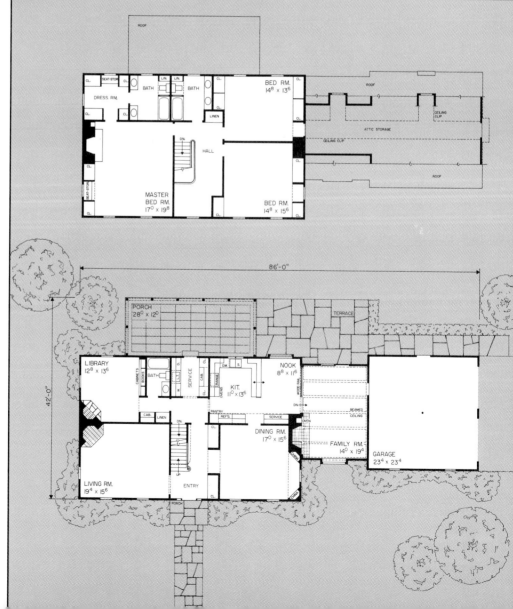

PLAN J2659

Type: Three-story
Style: Georgian
First floor: 1,023 square feet
Second floor: 1,003 square feet
Third floor: 476 square feet
Total: 2,502 square feet
Bedrooms: 3 + study
Bathrooms: 2½
Price schedule: B

The central hall of this Colonial leads to a living room with a fireplace, a cozy study, and back to a family kitchen. The adjacent dining room has an attractive bay window. The second floor houses three bedrooms; the third floor contains space for a studio and study.

In the dining room a gracious bay window overlooks the backyard.

PLAN J2980

Type: Three-story
Style: Georgian
First floor: 1,648 square feet
Second floor: 1,368 square feet
Third floor: 567 square feet
Total: 3,523 square feet
Bedrooms: 4 + library
Bathrooms: 3½
Price schedule: C

The facade of this late Georgian adaptation features Ionic columns, a Palladian window, and a pedimented gable. The centered foyer is flanked by living areas which flow around the fireplaces. Also note the sun room, laundry, and the bonus space of the third floor.

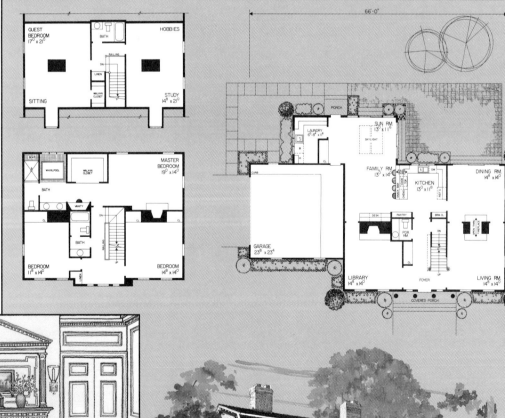

The living room boasts an ornate, pedimented fireplace.

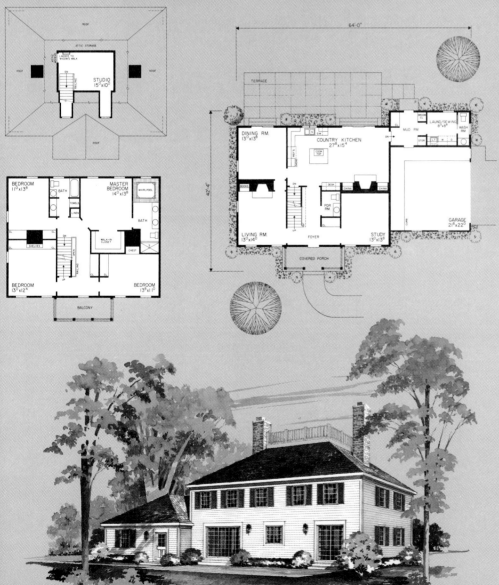

PLAN J2690

Type: Three-story
Style: Georgian
First floor: 1,559 square feet
Second floor: 1,344 square feet
Third floor: 176 square feet
Total: 3,103 square feet
Bedrooms: 4 + study
Bathrooms: 2½ + powder room
Price schedule: C

Reminiscent of homes in New England coastal towns, this Georgian features a balustraded roof deck, or "widow's walk," where captain's wives waited for signs of returning ships. Our updated floor plans include a country kitchen with an island cook top, a dining room, living room, and study on the first floor. The second-floor master suite has a whirlpool and walk-in closet. The third floor houses a studio and access to the widow's walk.

PLAN J2975

Type: Three-story
Style: Georgian
First floor: 1,656 square feet
Second floor: 1,440 square feet
Third floor: 715 square feet
Total: 3,811 square feet
Bedrooms: 4 + library
Bathrooms: 3½
Price schedule: D

The elegant facade of this stately home features a fan-light window over the front door, a second-story Palladian window, and arched dormers. Symmetrical double chimneys service four fireplaces in the living room, dining room, country kitchen, and library. Sliding glass doors in the dining room and country kitchen lead to the raised rear terrace. Upstairs, the master suite includes a fireplace in the bedroom and one in the bath. Also notice the whirlpool. The third floor houses a studio/hobby room and guest room.

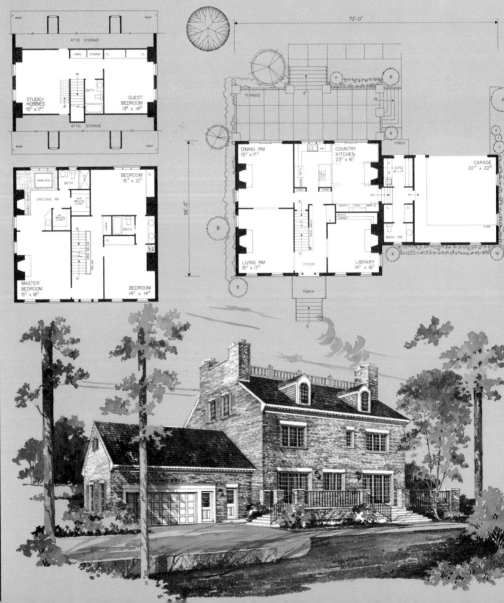

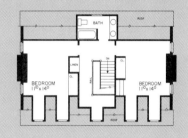

PLAN J2662

Type: Three-story
Style: Georgian
First floor: 1,735 square feet
Second floor: 1,075 square feet
Third floor: 746 square feet
Total: 3,556 square feet
Bedrooms: 5
Bathrooms: 3½
Price schedule: C

The matching wings of this handsome Georgian house a study and breakfast room, each with a fireplace. The first floor also includes a formal parlor, a dining room, gathering room, and country kitchen. Three bedrooms on the second floor and two on the third complete the plan.

The spacious country kitchen includes a built-in barbecue range.

109

PLAN J2683

Type: Two-story
Style: Georgian
First floor: 2,126 square feet
Second floor: 1,882 square feet
Total: 3,008 square feet
Bedrooms: 4 + study
Bathrooms: 2½
Price schedule: D

This historical Georgian home features modern conveniences and livability. The first floor includes a dining room, a study, and an enormous sunken gathering room, with a central fireplace. The spacious country kitchen features an island cooktop; the adjacent breakfast room opens to the terrace. Upstairs are four bedrooms; the sumptuous master suite has a luxurious bath with step-up tub, bedroom fireplace, and private, sunken lounge.

French doors with fanlight windows flood the gathering room with light.

PLAN J2192

Type: Three-story
Style: Georgian
First floor: 1,884 square feet,
Second floor: 1,521 square feet
Third floor: 808 square feet
(optional)
Total: 4,213 square feet
(with third floor)
Bedrooms: 3 + library
Bathrooms: 3½
Price schedule: D

This is surely a fine adaptation from the 18th Century when formality and elegance were bywords. Notice the authentic detailing and fine proportions. This gracious home has loads of living space. Flanking the foyer are spacious living and dining rooms. Adjacent to the dining room is a kitchen with a work island, and a large family room with a fireplace. There is also a corner library. Upstairs are three bedrooms. The plan also includes an optional third floor with space for a playroom, guest room, or work room.

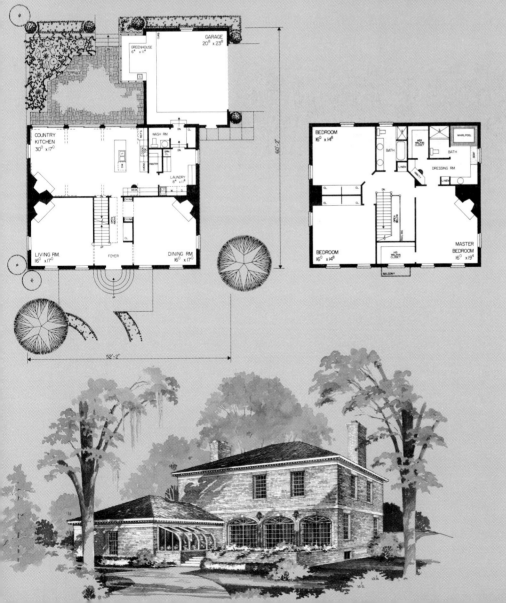

PLAN J2982

Type: Two-story
Style: Georgian
First floor: 1,584 square feet
Second floor: 1,513 square feet
Total: 3,097 square feet
Bedrooms: 3
Bathrooms: 2½
Price schedule: C

Reminiscent of Old Williamsburg, this Georgian mixes old-fashioned detail with modern convenience. Observe the massive twin chimneys, the cornice ornamentation, and the wrought-iron balcony sheltering the front door. The rectangular shape of this house will lead to economical construction costs. Inside, a huge country kitchen includes a work island, a fireplace, and a sun-splashed area for eating and relaxing. There's also access to the rear terrace. Don't miss the fireplace and whirlpool in the master bedroom and the greenhouse behind the garage.

PLAN J1852

Type: Two-story
Style: Georgian
First floor: 1,802 square feet
Second floor: 1,603 square feet
Total: 3,405 square feet
Bedrooms: 4
Bathrooms: 2½ + powder room
Price schedule: C

This is an impressive Georgian adaptation. Front-entrance detailing, window treatment, and masses of brick help put this house in a class of its own. The floor plan is a classic as well. A formal living room and dining room flank the front entry hall. The kitchen and breakfast nook are not far away, keeping entertaining work to a minimum. The large family room has built-in bookshelves and has access to a rear terrace. Two fireplaces with built-in wood boxes keep things warm and cozy. Four upstairs bedrooms include a master with window seat and bookshelves. Two other bedrooms feature large walk-in closets.

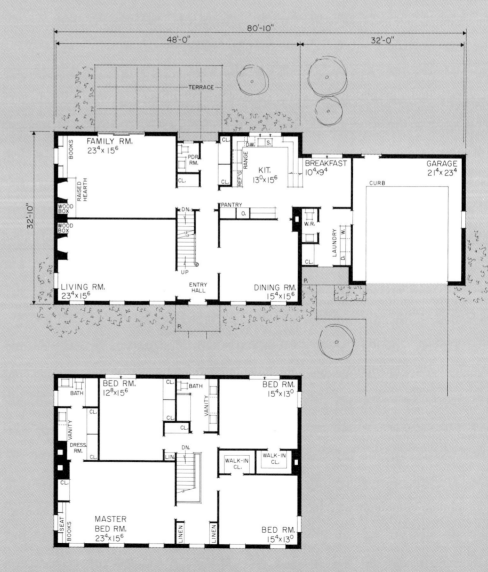

PLAN J1858

Type: Two-story
Style: Georgian
First floor: 1,794 square feet
Second floor: 1,474 square feet
Studio: 424 square feet
Total: 3,692 square feet
Bedrooms: 5 (includes studio)
Bathrooms: 3½ + powder room
Price schedule: C

From the delightful spacious front entry hall to the studio or maid's room over the garage, this home is unique all along the way. All the amenities required by today's lifestyles can be found here.

A sweeping staircase allows for a grand descent to the entry.

PLAN J2899

Type: Two-story
Style: Georgian
First floor: 1,685 square feet
Second floor: 1,437 square feet
Total: 3,122 square feet
Bedrooms: 4
Bathrooms: 2½ + powder room
Price schedule: C

This impressive Georgian home with massive twin chimneys and slender Roman Doric columns is authentic in its 18th-Century detailing. Inside, the home offers comfort and elegance with a living room, study with bay window, large formal dining room, breakfast room, and even a butler's pantry. Smooth traffic flow is enhanced by a central foyer that opens to stairs leading to the second story. This floor is thoughtfully zoned, too, with well-appointed master suite and three other bedrooms.

A large bay window in the private study becomes a grand stage for gorgeous backyard views.

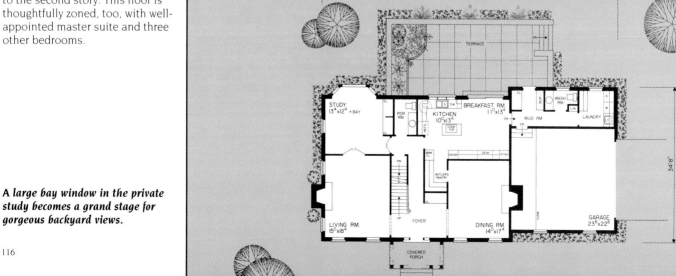

PLAN J2250

Type: Two-story
Style: Georgian
First floor: 1,442 square feet
Second floor: 1,404 square feet
Total: 2,846 square feet
Bedrooms: 4
Bathrooms: 3½
Price schedule: C

This home's roots go back to an earlier period in American architecture, yet its distinctive style remains a popular choice. The spacious front entry effectively separates formal and informal living zones — long living room to the left, family room and kitchen to the right. A dining room is conveniently placed in between. Notice the abundance of storage space in a walk-in closet in the entry and three closets in the garage. There are also two fireplaces for added enjoyment. Four bedrooms and three baths are on the second floor. Be sure to note the room-sized walk-in closet in the spacious master bedroom.

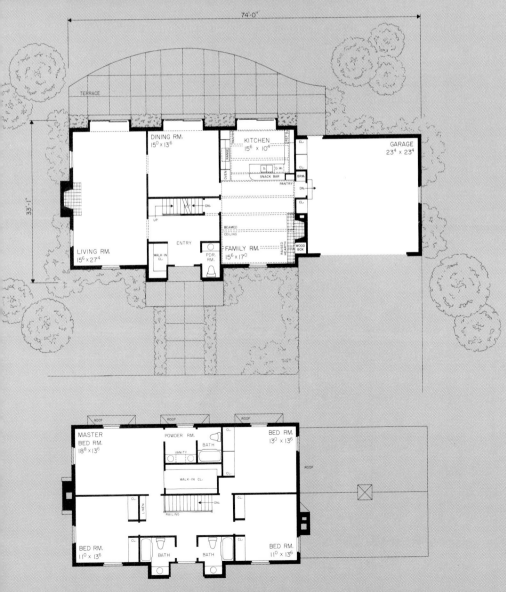

PLAN J1767

Type: Two-story
Style: Georgian
First floor: 1,510 square feet
Second floor: 1,406 square feet
Total: 2,916 square feet
Bedrooms: 4
Bathrooms: 2½ + powder room
Price schedule: C

Symmetry speaks clearly in this Georgian adaptation. Window treatment, paired chimneys, and a columned front porch all provide special touches. Inside living revolves around the central kitchen and eating nook. A pass-through to the family room and large pantry add efficiency. A house-wide terrace can be reached at two points by sliding glass doors. For even more convenience, a mud room with attached washroom is located just off the garage (note also the large storage area). A second-floor master suite has two walk-in closets.

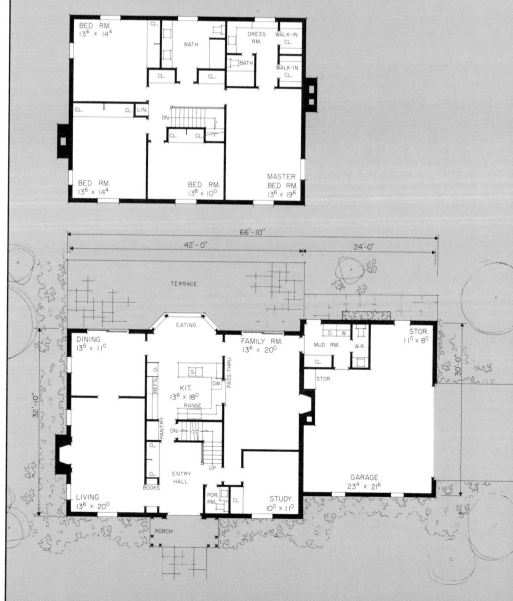

PLAN J2139

Type: Two-story
Style: Georgian
First floor: 1,581 square feet
Second floor: 991 square feet
Total: 2,572 square feet
Bedrooms: 4
Bathrooms: 2½
Price schedule: B

Double wings serve their purpose as a visual treat and floor plan feature in this grand brick home. A garage takes up one wing and formal living areas are in the other. A well-designed kitchen area has many built-in amenities and a pass-through to the breakfast nook. Reach a rear terrace through sliding glass doors in each of the two eating areas. A bonus room is set aside as an office or hobby room and is close to a washroom for easy clean-ups. Upstairs bedrooms handle sleeping accommodations for the whole family.

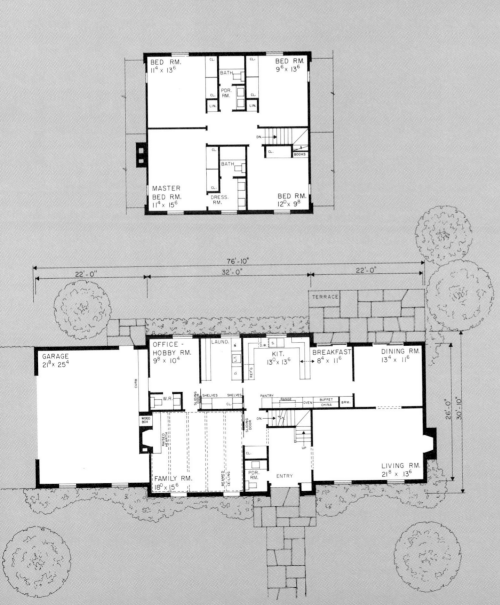

PLAN J2889

Type: Two-story
Style: Georgian
First floor: 2,529 square feet
Second floor: 1,872 square feet
Total: 4,401 square feet
Bedrooms: 4
Bathrooms: 3½
Price schedule: D

This is truly classical Georgian design at its best. Some of the exterior highlights of this two-story include the pediment gable with cornice work and dentils, the beautifully proportioned columns, the front door detailing and the window treatment. Behind the facade of this design is an equally elegant interior. The large receiving hall is graced by two curving staircases and opens to the formal living and dining rooms. Beyond the living room is the study. Large informal occasions will be enjoyed in the spacious gathering room. It has a centered fireplace flanked by windows on each side. An efficient work center with kitchen, breakfast room, washroom, and laundry rounds out the first floor. Three bedrooms and two full baths are joined by the feature-filled master bedroom on the second floor.

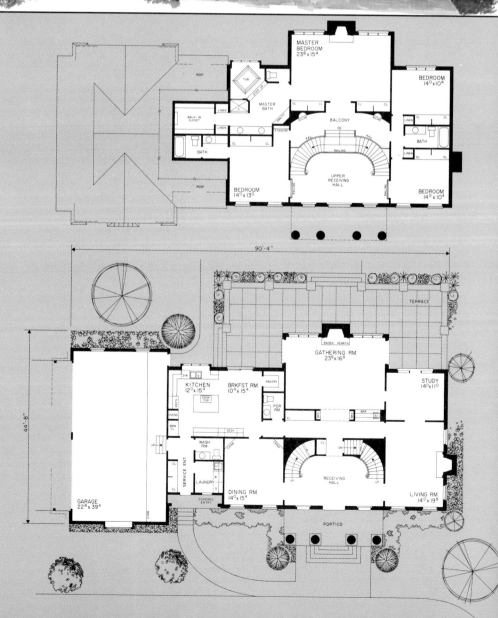

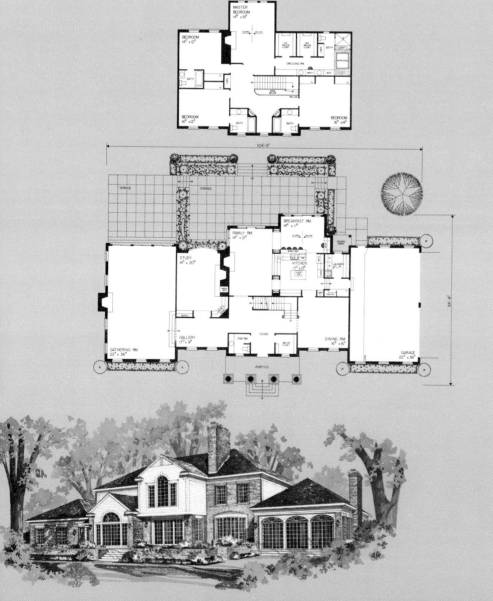

PLAN J2984

Type: Two-story
Style: Georgian
First floor: 3,116 square feet
Second floor: 1,997 square feet
Total: 5,113 square feet
Bedrooms: 4
Bathrooms: 4½
Price schedule: E

An echo of Whitehall, built in 1765 in Anne Arundel County, Maryland, resounds in this home. Its classic symmetry and columned facade herald a grand interior. There's no lack of space whether entertaining formally or just enjoying a family get-together, and all are kept cozy with fireplaces in the gathering room, study, and family room. An island kitchen with attached breakfast room handily serves the nearby dining room. Four second-floor bedrooms include a large master suite with another fireplace, a whirlpool, and His and Hers closets in the bath. Three more full baths are on this floor.

PLAN J2283

Type: Two-story
Style: Federal
First floor: 1,559 square feet
Second floor: 1,404 square feet
Total: 2,963 square feet
Bedrooms: 4
Bathrooms: 2½ + powder room
Price schedule: C

This elegant two-story home is reminiscent of the stately character of Federal architecture during an earlier period in our history. The home is replete with exquisite detailing. Features that make this design unique and appealing include cornice work, pediment gable, dentils, brick quoins at the corners, beautifully proportioned columns, front door detailing, window treatment, and massive twin chimneys. All four bedrooms are located upstairs away from other household traffic and noise. Notice the kitchen nook with bay window and adjoining formal dining area.

PLAN J2230

Type: Two-story
Style: Georgian
First floor: 2,288 square feet
Second floor: 1,863 square feet
Total: 4,151 square feet
Bedrooms: 3
Bathrooms: 4
Price schedule: D

The gracefulness and appeal of this Southern adaptation will be everlasting. The imposing two-story portico is truly dramatic. Notice the authentic detailing of the tapered Doric columns, the balustraded roof deck, the denticulated cornice, the front entrance and the shuttered windows. The architecture of the rear is no less appealing with its formal symmetry and smaller Doric portico. The impressive interior of this two-story houses a total of 4,151 square feet. The spacious, formal front entrance hall provides a fitting introduction to the scale and elegance of the interior.

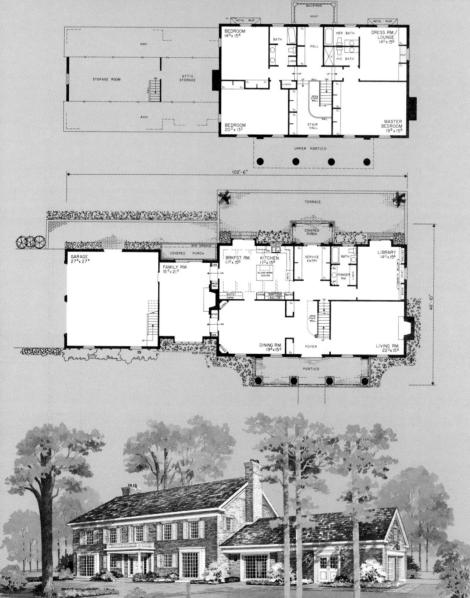

PLAN J2368

Type: Two-story
Style: Georgian
First floor: 1,592 square feet
Second floor: 1,255 square feet
Total: 2,847 square feet
Bedrooms: 4
Bathrooms: 2½
Price schedule: C

A pleasing combination of roof heights and exterior materials highlight the facade of this traditional two-story. The interior floor plan is every bit as delightful. Arranged around the entrance hall, powder room, and laundry are spacious living and working areas: living room, dining room, and kitchen with nook. The family room joins the garage to the main part of the house. The upstairs sleeping zone is comprised of four bedrooms and two baths. Added touches to livability include two fireplaces and a lovely flagstone terrace off the family room.

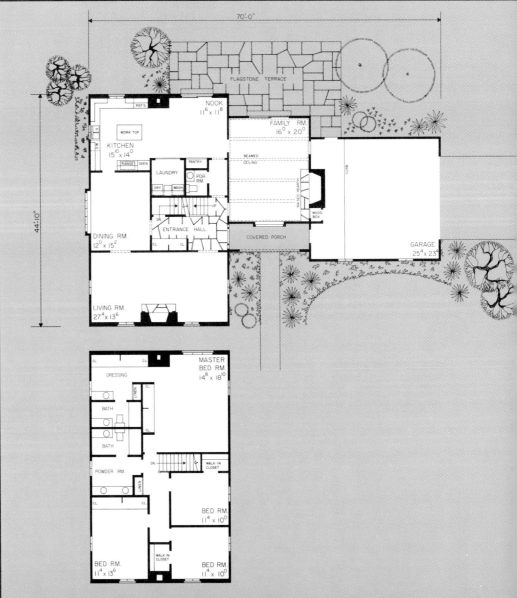

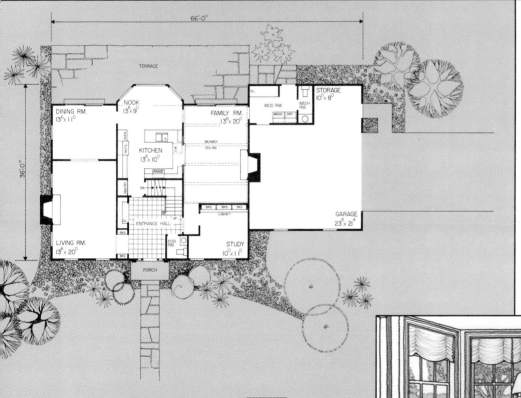

PLAN J2610

Type: Two-story
Style: Georgian
First floor: 1,505 square feet
Second floor: 1,344 square feet
Total: 2,849 square feet
Bedrooms: 4
Bathrooms: 2½ + powder room
Price schedule: C

Recalling images of a New England yesteryear, this wonderful traditional keeps its heritage alive with multi-paned windows, entrance detailing, narrow horizontal siding with corner boards, and two chimneys.

A sunny bay window adds charm to the breakfast nook.

PLAN J2693

Type: One-story
Style: Georgian
Square footage: 3,462
Bedrooms: 3 or 4 (sewing room)
Bathrooms: 3½
Price schedule: D

Though containing a thoroughly updated interior, this manor is reminiscent of historic Rose Hill, built in 1818 in Lexington, Kentucky. Notice the symmetry in four chimney stacks and four Ionic columns.

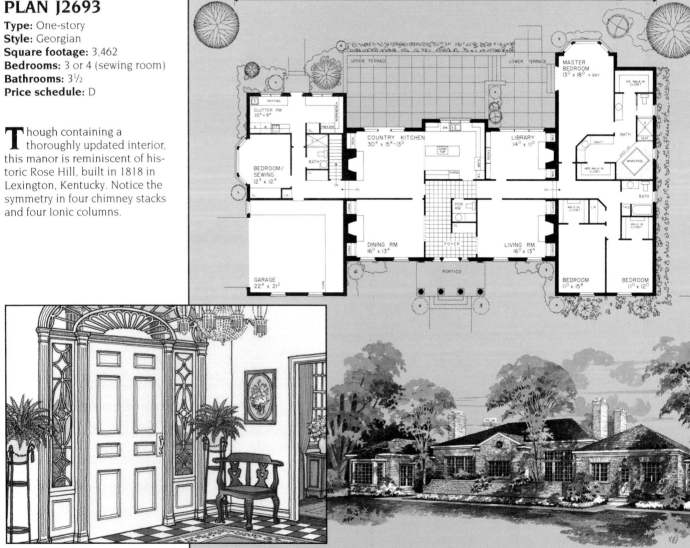

Detailed glasswork lights the foyer for guests.

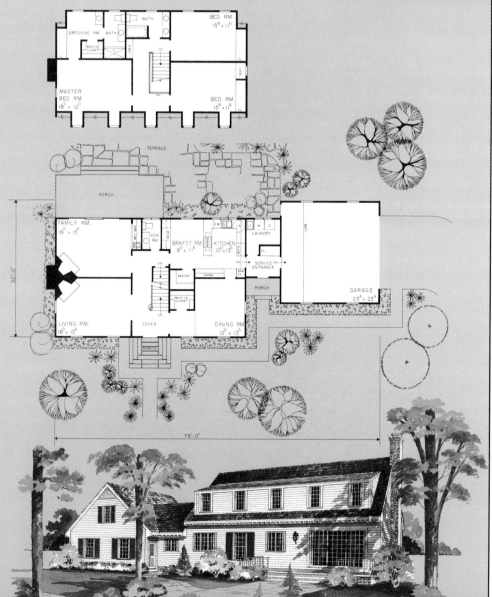

PLAN J2520

Type: Two-story
Style: Tidewater
First floor: 1,419 square feet
Second floor: 1,040 square feet
Total: 2,459 square feet
Bedrooms: 3
Bathrooms: 2½
Price schedule: B

A charming adaptation shows characteristic influences from Tidewater, Virginia. The classic floor plan — living and dining rooms to the front, family room and kitchen/breakfast room to the rear — will serve the needs of all family activities. A large porch, reached from the family room, gives way to a terrace, enhancing outdoor fun. Twin corner fireplaces share a chimney stack. The fine master bedroom on the second floor has a full bath and is joined by two more bedrooms and a full bath.

PLAN J2688

Type: Two-story
Style: Tidewater
First floor: 1,588 square feet
Second floor: 1,101 square feet
Total: 2,689 square feet
Bedrooms: 3
Bathrooms: 2½
Price schedule: B

From country kitchen to quiet library, this design offers excellent livability. It features many built-ins, a rear terrace area, second-story dormer windows, and two fireplaces.

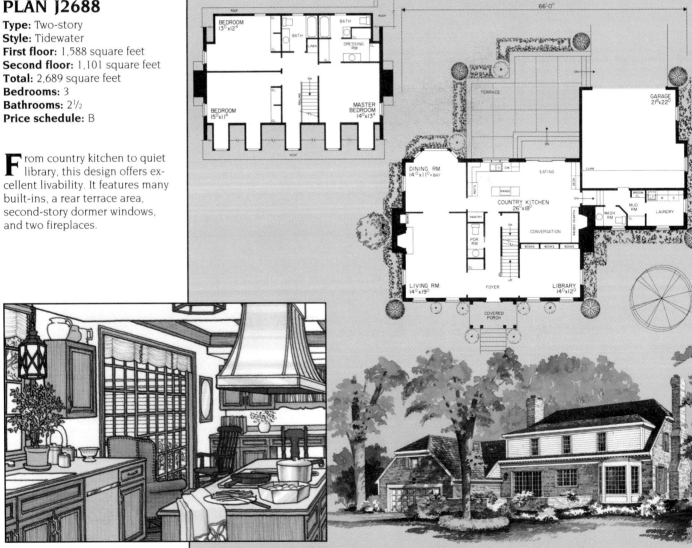

*Sliding glass doors are an
invitation to enjoy the view.*

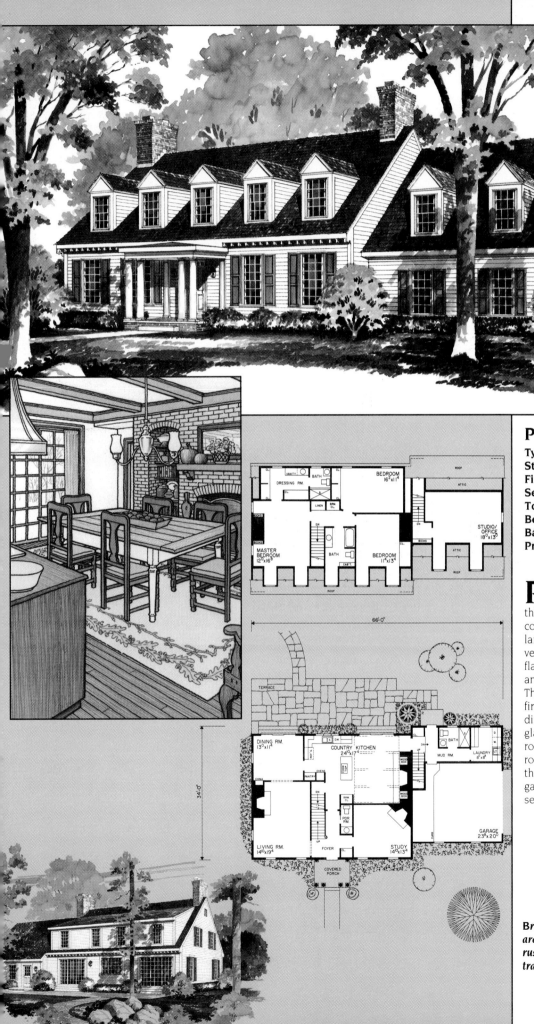

PLAN J2684

Type: Two-story
Style: Tidewater
First floor: 1,600 square feet
Second floor: 1,498 square feet
Total: 3,098 square feet
Bedrooms: 3
Bathrooms: 3½
Price schedule: C

Pretty architectural detailing is one of the first attractions of this fine home. Its many interior considerations confirm its popularity. The center foyer, with conveniently placed powder room, is flanked by a formal living room and study. Both have fireplaces. The country kitchen, with another fireplace, is adjacent to a formal dining room. Look for sliding glass doors to the terrace in both rooms. Besides the three bedrooms and two baths upstairs, there is a studio/office over the garage. The mud room and bath serve this area nicely.

Brick accents in a country kitchen are a suitable complement to the rustic charm of hardwood floors and traditional furnishings.

PLAN J2638

Type: Two-story
Style: Tidewater
First floor: 1,836 square feet
Second floor: 1,323 square feet
Total: 3,159 square feet
Bedrooms: 3 (optional 4)
Bathrooms: 2½
Price schedule: C

The brick facade of this two-story represents the mid-18th Century design concept. It has a steeply pitched roof which is broken at each end by two large chimneys and by pedimented dormers. The floor plan is highly symmetrical. The entrance hall becomes a central foyer through the width of the house. To either side are a dining room, country kitchen, living room, and family room. Each has a fireplace. Upstairs are sleeping quarters that can be configured in a three or four bedroom plan — blueprints include details for both. Close inspection reveals many built-ins and thoughtful amenities.

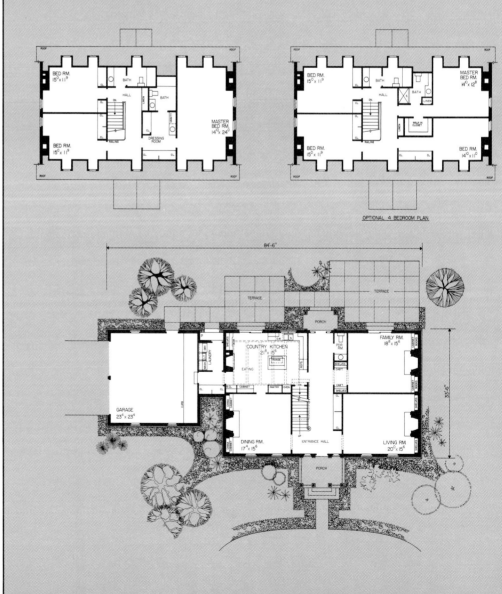

OPTIONAL 4 BEDROOM PLAN

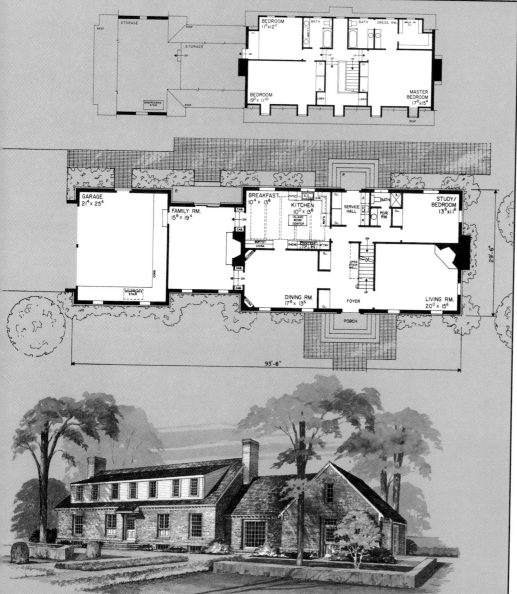

PLAN J2132

Type: Two-story
Style: Tidewater
First floor: 1,958 square feet
Second floor: 1,305 square feet
Total: 3,263 square feet
Bedrooms: 3 or 4 (study)
Bathrooms: 3
Price schedule: C

Nineteenth-Century heritage in a 20th-Century floor plan! Among the many special components of this home are two fireplaces, built-in china cabinet/buffet and barbecue in kitchen, sunken family room, and a study that can also be used as a fourth bedroom. A master suite on the second floor features double vanities, a large walk-in closet, and a dressing room. Two more bedrooms on this floor share a full bath with double vanities. Distinctive dormer windows are a quaint addition as are the step-up porches at front and rear entries. There's no lack of storage, either, with huge spaces over the family room and garage.

PLAN J2695

Type: Two-story
Style: Tidewater
First floor: 2,058 square feet
Second floor: 1,181 square feet
Total: 3,239 square feet
Bedrooms: 4
Bathrooms: 3½
Price schedule: C

The gambrel roof, projecting dormers, and end chimneys of this Colonial home are highly identifiable architectural features of the 18th Century Tidewater house. The floor plan allows for master suite upstairs or downstairs in equal fashion.

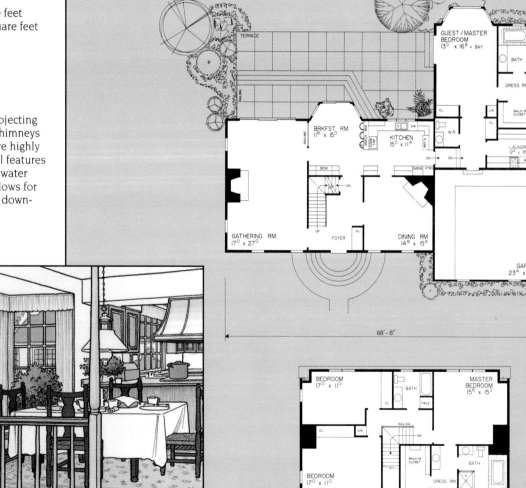

The breakfast room and kitchen allow space for enjoying meals.

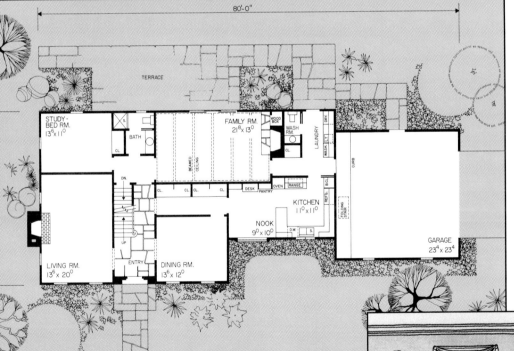

PLAN J2631

Type: Two-story
Style: Tidewater
First floor: 1,634 square feet
Second floor: 1,011 square feet
Total: 2,645 square feet
Bedrooms: 3 or 4 (study)
Bathrooms: 3½
Price schedule: B

Exceptional traffic efficiency is a plus in this family plan. All living areas are easily accessible from the main hall. Three bedrooms upstairs are complemented by an optional fourth on the first floor which may also serve as a study.

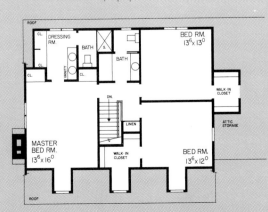

Traditional furnishings promote a living room design.

133

PLAN J2691

Type: Two-story
Style: Tidewater
First floor: 1,550 square feet
Second floor: 1,142 square feet
Total: 2,692 square feet
Bedrooms: 3
Bathrooms: 2½
Price schedule: B

This compact Virginia manor can trace its styling heritage to the 18th Century. Inside, the design packs loads of livability. On either side of the foyer visitors find a formal parlor and a gathering room, each with matching corner fireplaces. To the rear are an ample country kitchen and a dining room with a bay window overlooking the back yard. The second floor houses three big bedrooms and two full baths. The built-in desk in the stair hall makes a quiet work area. Also notice the abundant closet space on the second floor.

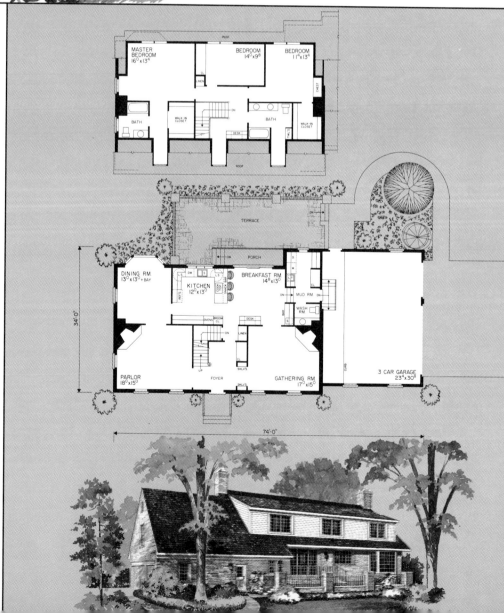

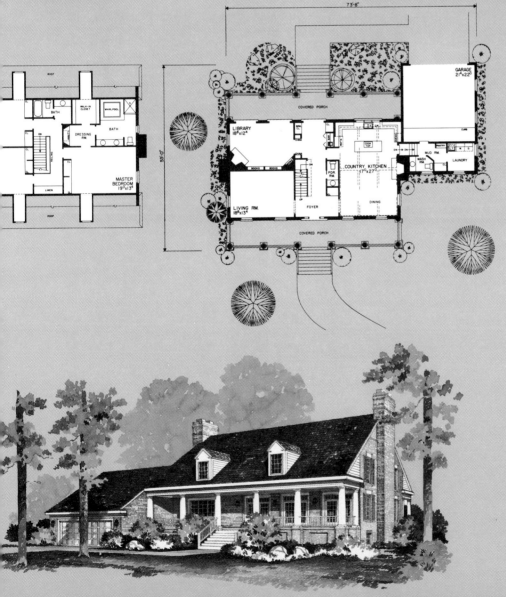

PLAN J2686

Type: Two-story
Style: Tidewater
First floor: 1,683 square feet
Second floor: 1,541 square feet
Total: 3,224 square feet
Bedrooms: 3 + library
Bathrooms: 2½ + powder room
Price schedule: C

This design has its roots in the South with its front and rear covered porches and Greek Revival columns. The entrance hall leads all the way to the rear porch. To the left are the living room and the library with its corner fireplace and built-in bookshelves. To the right, the enormous country kitchen and dining area stretch the full depth of the house. Next to the kitchen are the mud room, laundry, and a washroom. Upstairs, three spacious bedrooms include a master suite with dressing room and whirlpool. There's also plenty of closet space.

PLAN J2919

Type: Two-story
Style: Tidewater
First floor: 1,436 square feet
Second floor: 907 square feet
Total: 2,343 square feet
Bedrooms: 2 + library
Bathrooms: 2½
Price schedule: B

Big things frequently come in little packages. This modest 1½-story house has a charming character all its own. Typical of Southern plantation houses, this design features a raised first floor. Off the centered foyer are the living room and library with built-in bookshelves. To the rear are the dining room with a bay window and a spacious country kitchen which boasts a corner fireplace. The second floor houses two bedrooms, each with its own bath. Also notice the cozy lounge — perfect for curling up with a book. Don't miss the storage areas under the eaves.

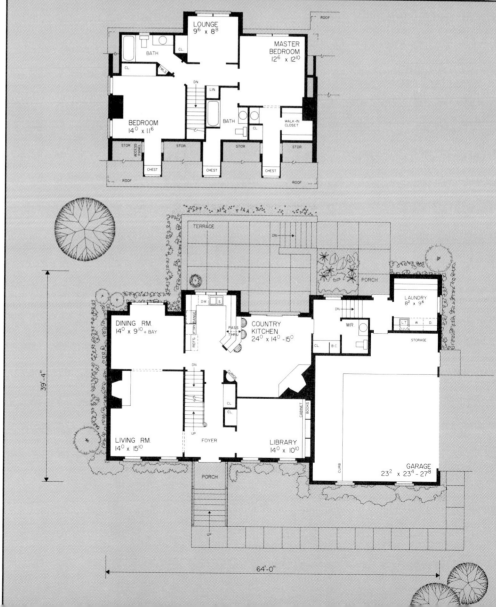

PLAN J2898

Type: Two-story
Style: Greek Revival
First floor: 1,619 square feet
Second floor: 1,723 square feet
Total: 3,342 square feet
Bedrooms: 4 + lounge
Bathrooms: 3½
Price schedule: C

Four soaring Doric columns highlight the exterior of this Greek Revival dwelling. Inside, the foyer leads straight back to the two-story gathering room. The front parlor provides additional living space. A dining room and spacious kitchen round out the first floor. Four bedrooms upstairs include a large master suite with a dressing room and exercise area. Also notice the balcony lounge above the gathering room.

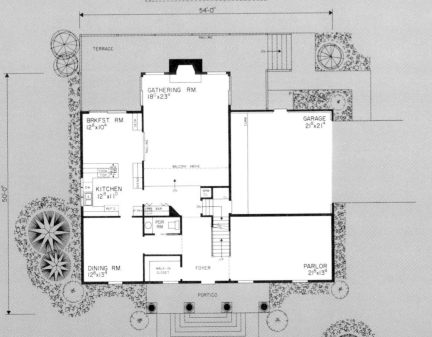

PLAN J2184

Type: Two-story
Style: Greek Revival
First floor: 1,999 square feet
Second floor: 1,288 square feet
Total: 3,287 square feet
Bedrooms: 3 + library
Bathrooms: 3
Price schedule: C

The Greek facade of this home looks back to another era; the interior, however, reflects modern living. The grand entrance hall leads left into the living room and connecting dining room. Adjacent are a large kitchen and an enormous family room and breakfast area. Also notice the snack bar pass-through, the built-in barbecue, china cabinet, and planning desk in this modern, efficient kitchen. Also downstairs, discover a laundry room and full bath. Up the curving staircase are two bedrooms and the master suite with dressing room and lounge. Also note the private balcony.

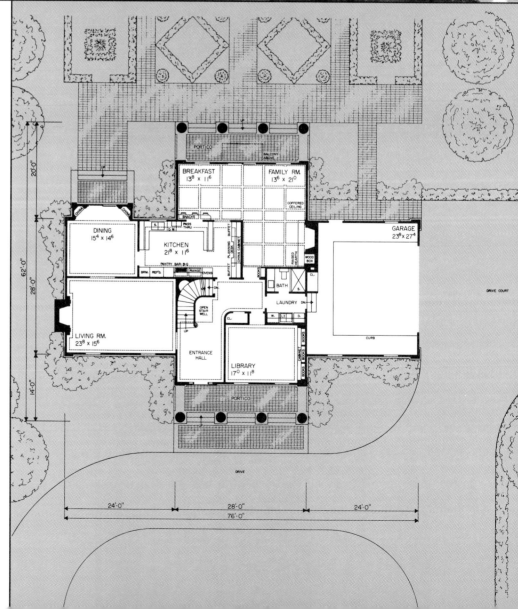

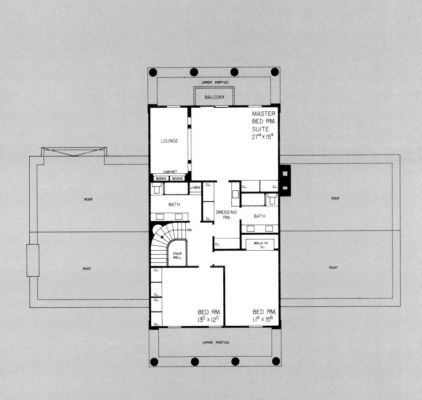

PLAN J2696

Type: Two-story
Style: Greek Revival
First floor: 2,217 square feet
Second floor: 1,962 square feet
Total: 4,179 square feet
Bedrooms: 4 + media room
Bathrooms: 3½ + powder room
Price schedule: D

This Greek Revival design pairs a gracious facade with an equally elegant interior. The grand entrance foyer features a curving staircase and leads to the living room, dining room, media room, and the sunny morning room. Upstairs are four bedrooms.

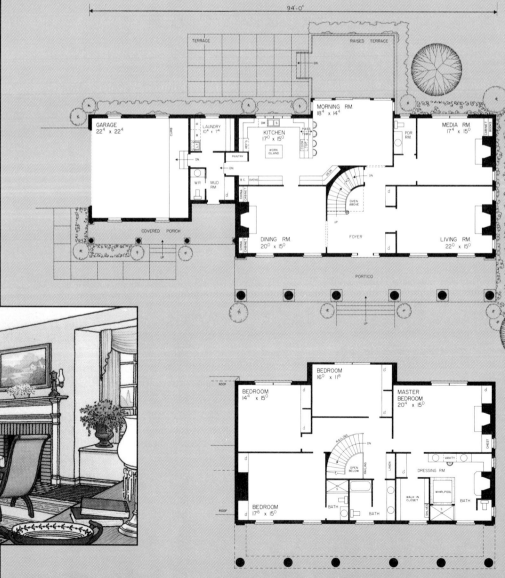

A fireplace makes the master bedroom a warm, cozy retreat.

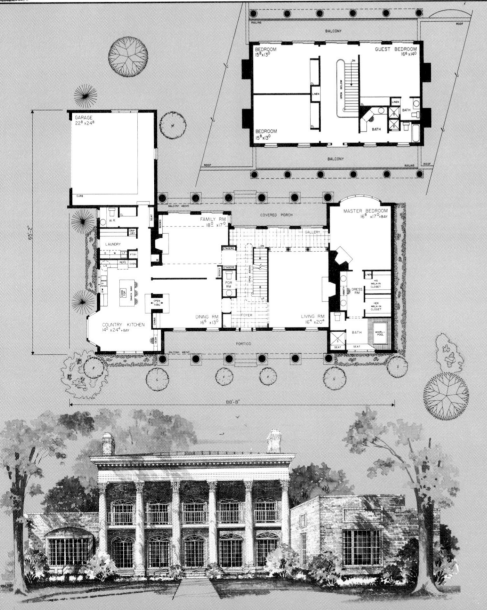

PLAN J2987

Type: Two-story
Style: Greek Revival
First floor: 2,822 square feet
Second floor: 1,335 square feet
Total: 4,157 square feet
Bedrooms: 4
Bathrooms: 3 1/2 + powder room
Price schedule: D

Andrew Jackson's dream of white-pillared splendor resulted in the building of his pride, The Hermitage, near Nashville, Tennessee. The essence of that grand dream is recaptured in this modern variation. A provocative use of dramatic features sets this home apart from the rest. Matching columns of twin chimneys tower over the one-story wings; six Corinthian columns highlight the facade. The elegant interior includes spacious living, dining, and family rooms, a country kitchen, a sunny gallery, and a master bedroom with a fireplace and a whirlpool. Don't miss the front and rear balconies.

PLAN J2668

Type: Two-story
Style: Greek Revival
First floor: 1,206 square feet
Second floor: 1,254 square feet
Total: 2,460 square feet
Bedrooms: 4 + library
Bathrooms: 2½
Price schedule: B

This elegant exterior houses a very livable plan. The spacious country kitchen with its built-ins and island cook top will make preparing meals a pleasure. The dining room is adjacent for convenience in serving. The two-story great room will be the center of family activities. Imagine entertaining in this dramatic room. Upstairs are a balcony lounge and four bedrooms.

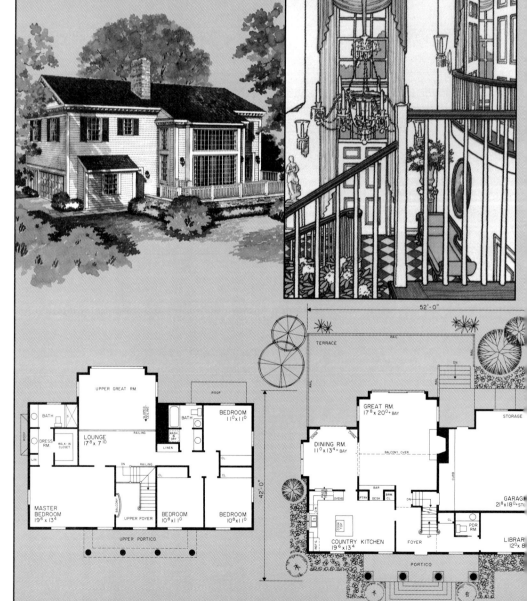

A large window floods the two-story foyer with light.

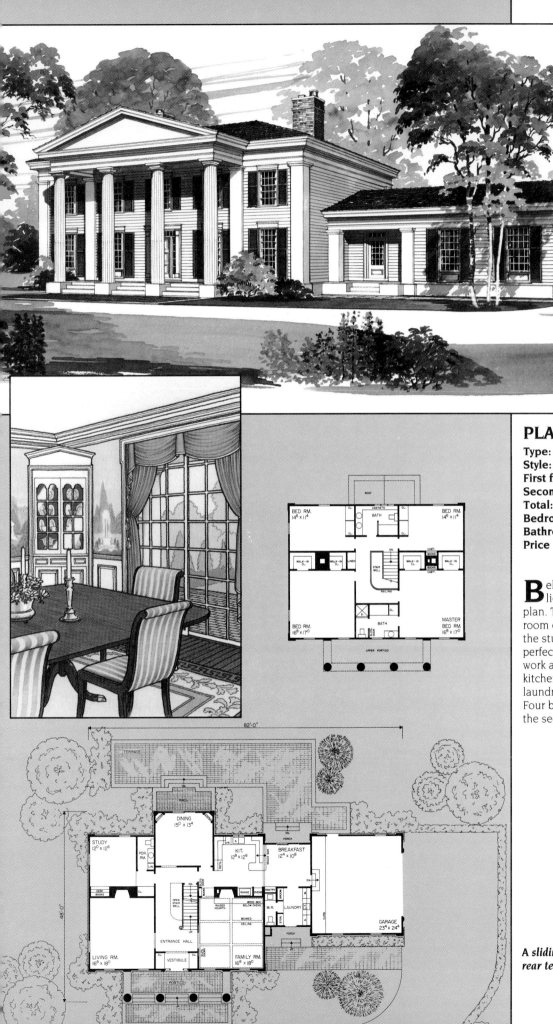

PLAN J2185

Type: Two-story
Style: Greek Revival
First floor: 1,916 square feet
Second floor: 1,564 square feet
Total: 3,480 square feet
Bedrooms: 4 + study
Bathrooms: 2½ + powder room
Price schedule: C

Behind this grand facade lies a hard-working floor plan. The living room and dining room can function formally while the study and family room are perfect for family relaxation. The work area contains a spacious kitchen with breakfast room, a laundry room, and a wash room. Four bedrooms are housed on the second floor.

A sliding glass door opens onto the rear terrace.

PLAN J2681

Type: Two-story
Style: Greek Revival
First floor: 1,350 square feet
Second floor: 1,224 square feet
Total: 2,574 square feet
Bedrooms: 3
Bathrooms: 2½
Price schedule: B

Greek Revival pilasters separate this farmhouse from the rest. Adjacent to the foyer are the formal parlor and the family room/living room. To the rear is a spacious kitchen and a dining room with a bay window.

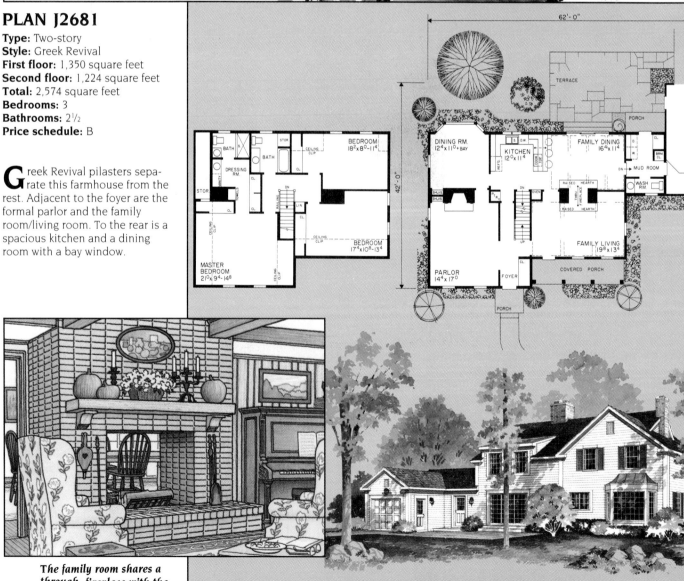

The family room shares a through-fireplace with the kitchen.

PLAN J2979

Type: Two-story
Style: Greek Revival
First floor: 1,440 square feet
Second floor: 1,394 square feet
Total: 2,834 square feet
Bedrooms: 4 + study
Bathrooms: 3½
Price schedule: C

Perfect for a narrow site, this Greek Revival adaptation delivers big-house livability. There are formal living and dining rooms for entertaining. The country kitchen is a multi-purpose room with its efficient work area and relaxing corner by the raised-hearth fireplace. The adjacent terrace provides a spot for outdoor meals. A corner study with a fireplace is a cozy retreat. The four-bedroom upstairs includes a spacious master bedroom which features a fireplace, a private balcony, and a whirlpool. Don't miss the greenhouse behind the garage.

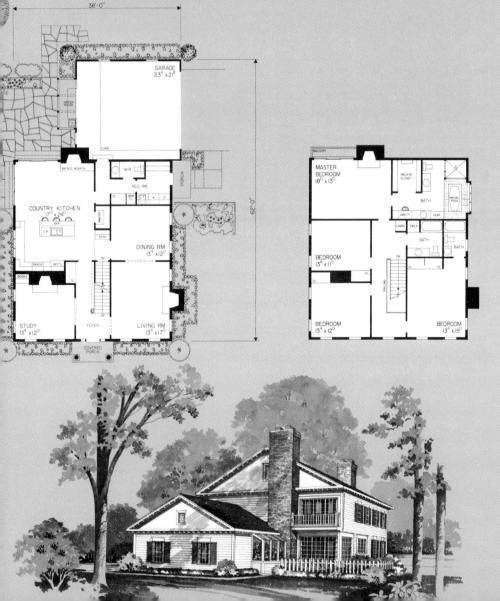

PLAN J2977

Type: Two-story
Style: Greek Revival
First floor: 4,104 square feet
Second floor: 979 square feet
Total: 5,083 square feet
Bedrooms: 4 + library
Bathrooms: 4½
Price schedule: D

Both front and rear facades of this elegant brick manor depict classic symmetry. A columned, Greek entry opens to an impressive two-story foyer. Fireplaces, built-in shelves, and cabinets highlight each of the four main gathering areas: living room, dining room, family room, and library. The kitchen features a handy work island and snack bar. The master suite is located in its own wing and has a private atrium entrance and lounge/exercise room. A fifth fireplace graces the master bedroom and additional features include His and Hers walk-in closets, built-in vanity, and whirlpool bath. Two bedrooms, each with private bath and double walk-in closets, are located on the second floor.

Multi-pane windows drench the family room with sunlight.

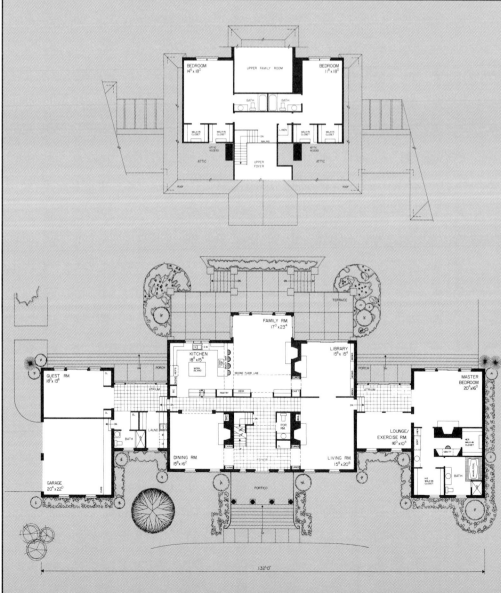

PLAN J2663

Type: Two-story
Style: Greek Revival
First floor: 1,344 square feet
Second floor: 947 square feet
Total: 2,291 square feet
Bedrooms: 3
Bathrooms: 2½
Price schedule: B

While the exterior comes from yesteryear, the floor plan of this design serves today's active family. The enormous gathering room is a multi-purpose living area, conveniently adjacent to the kitchen. There are three bedrooms upstairs with two full baths.

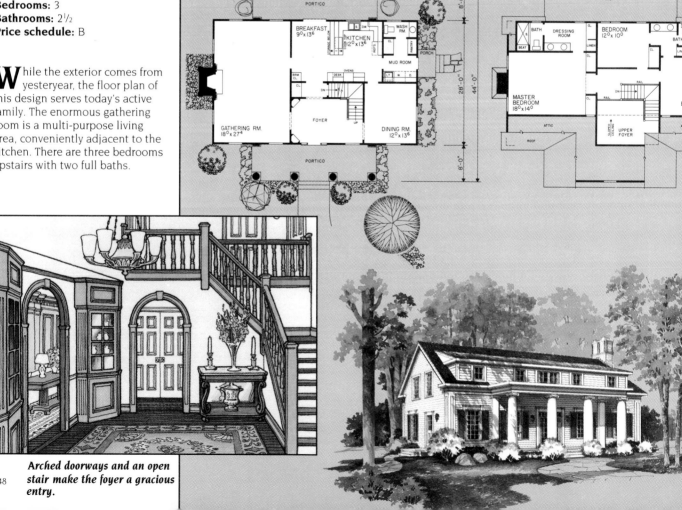

Arched doorways and an open stair make the foyer a gracious entry.

PLAN J2633

Type: Three-story
Style: Farmhouse
First floor: 1,338 square feet
Second floor: 1,200 square feet
Third floor: 506 square feet
Total: 3,044 square feet
Bedrooms: 4 + study
Bathrooms: 2½
Price schedule: C

This pleasing brick farmhouse features a very livable floor plan. The living room and dining room provide for formal occasions. The open kitchen and family room create a large area for working and relaxing together. Upstairs are four bedrooms. The third floor can be used as a study or studio.

The U-shaped kitchen has a convenient pass-through to the family room.

PLAN J2542

Type: Two-story
Style: Farmhouse
First floor: 2,025 square feet
Second floor: 1,726 square feet
Total: 3,751 square feet
Bedrooms: 4 + lounge
Bathrooms: 2½ + powder room
Price schedule: D

This fieldstone farmhouse has its roots in the countryside of Pennsylvania. Part of its charm includes its various additions, traditionally added as fortunes increased. Study the outstanding livability of this plan. The entrance hall routes traffic to all areas. To the left are the formal living room and dining room, each with a corner fireplace. Adjacent is the powder room and the spacious kitchen with island work center and eating nook. The comfortable family room with beamed ceiling and fireplace is one step down from the kitchen. Also notice the quiet haven of the study and the four-bedroom upstairs.

The family room boasts a beamed ceiling and a large stone fireplace.

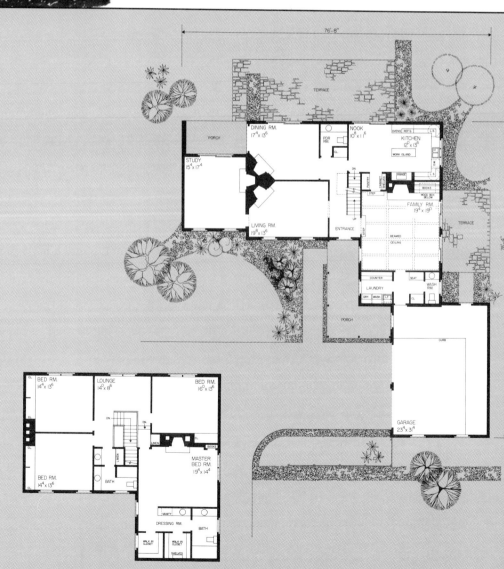

PLAN J2685

Type: Two-story
Style: Farmhouse
First floor: 1,605 square feet
Second floor: 1,561 square feet
Total: 3,166 square feet
Bedrooms: 4
Bathrooms: 2½
Price schedule: C

The stone exterior of this house recalls the Colonial farmhouses of Valley Forge. Spaciously planned to serve today's family, the design features a country kitchen as the hub of family life. Sleeping facilities include a master suite with its own private circular staircase.

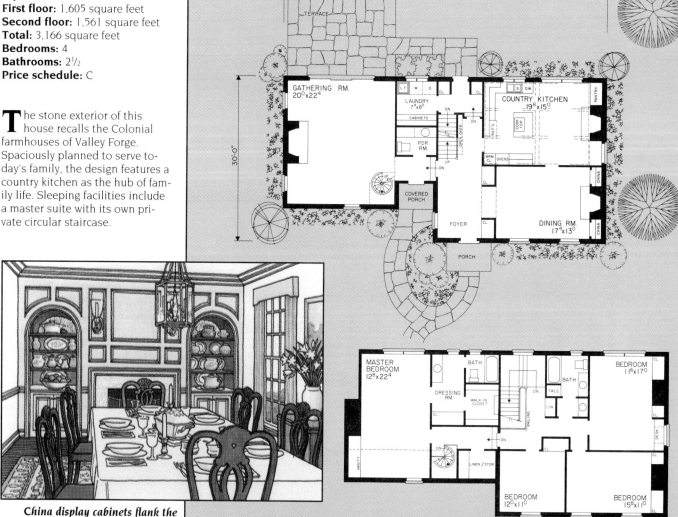

China display cabinets flank the fireplace in the dining room.

PLAN J2976

Type: Two-story
Style: Farmhouse
First floor: 1,786 square feet
Second floor: 1,260 square feet
Total: 3,046 square feet
Bedrooms: 3 + study
Bathrooms: 2½
Price schedule: C

Traditional styling meets modern livability in this design. The exterior brings to mind the stone houses of Bucks County, Pennsylvania while the well-planned interior reflects the needs of today's family. Flanking the foyer are formal living and dining rooms, each with fireplace. The living room also contains a windowed music alcove. Adjacent to the kitchen is a spacious breakfast room with an enormous bay window. Away from bustle and noise, the sunken study with fireplace offers a retreat. Also notice the enormous rear terrace — perfect for entertaining or relaxing. The three-bedroom upstairs features nice-sized rooms and a fourth fireplace. Note the laundry.

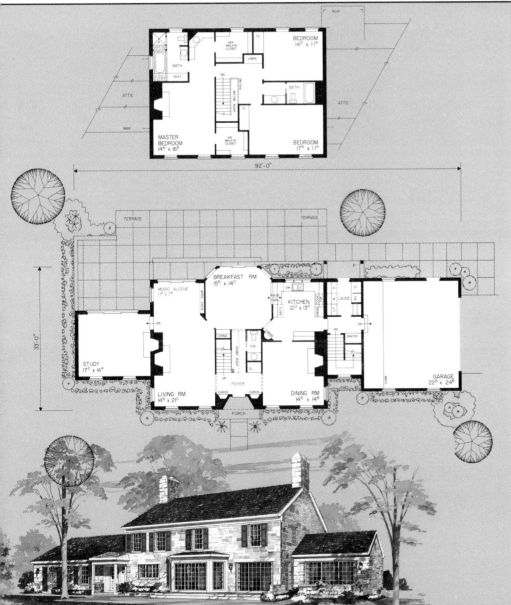

PLAN J2306

Type: Two-story
Style: Farmhouse
First floor: 1,425 square feet
Second floor: 1,464 square feet
Total: 2,889 square feet
Bedrooms: 4
Bathrooms: 2½ + powder room
Price schedule: C

What a delightful Farmhouse adaptation! The total livability it offers is outstanding; study this plan closely. A large living room occupies the left wing, away from bustle and noise. To the rear and adjacent to the kitchen is the formal dining room with bow window overlooking the backyard. The efficient kitchen includes a breakfast area. The beamed-ceilinged family room connects to the kitchen and entrance hall. Note the spaciousness of these rooms. Four bedrooms are housed upstairs; the master bedroom has a fireplace and a dressing room.

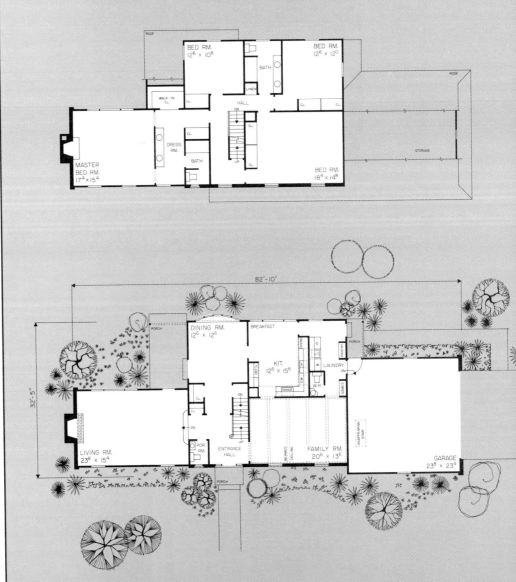

PLAN J2223

Type: Two-story
Style: Farmhouse
First floor: 1,266 square feet
Second floor: 1,232 square feet
Total: 2,498 square feet
Bedrooms: 4 or 5 (optional study)
Bathrooms: 2½
Price schedule: B

This traditional farmhouse features an efficient floor plan. The family room and living room are off the entrance hall. The dining room boasts a bay window and is next to the kitchen. One of the five upstairs bedrooms can serve as a convenient study.

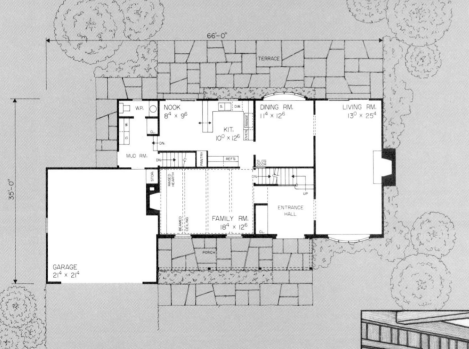

The family room features a raised-hearth fireplace.

PLAN J2963

Type: Two-story
Style: Farmhouse
First floor: 2,028 square feet
Second floor: 1,516 square feet
Total: 3,544 square feet
Bedrooms: 3 or 4
(optional nursery)
Bathrooms: 2½ + powder room
Price schedule: D

This brick Colonial includes many features our forefathers would envy. Notice the bay windows in the living room, the media room, and kitchen. There's also an island cook top in the kitchen. Four bedrooms upstairs include a master suite with His and Hers closets and a whirlpool.

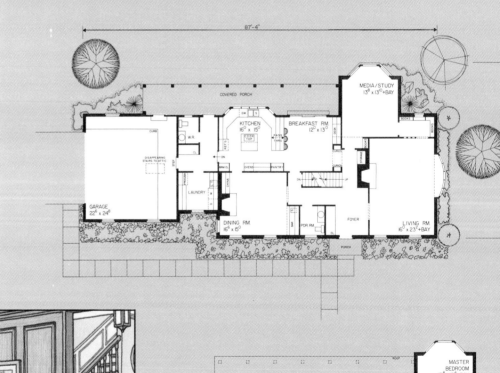

The spacious wood-paneled living room is located off the entry.

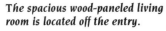

PLAN J2344

Type: Two-story
Style: Farmhouse
First floor: 1,516 square feet
Second floor: 1,794 square feet
Total: 3,310 square feet
Bedrooms: 4 + library
Bathrooms: 3½ + powder room
Price schedule: C

This spacious farmhouse features a livable, carefully zoned floor plan. The side entrance routes traffic to the enormous living room on the left and family room on the right. Tucked in a corner behind the living room, the library offers a quiet haven. The large U-shaped kitchen is conveniently adjacent to the dining room and opens onto the covered front porch. Notice the separate laundry room. The expansive upstairs includes three bedrooms and a study in one section; the private master suite is off by itself and has its own lounge.

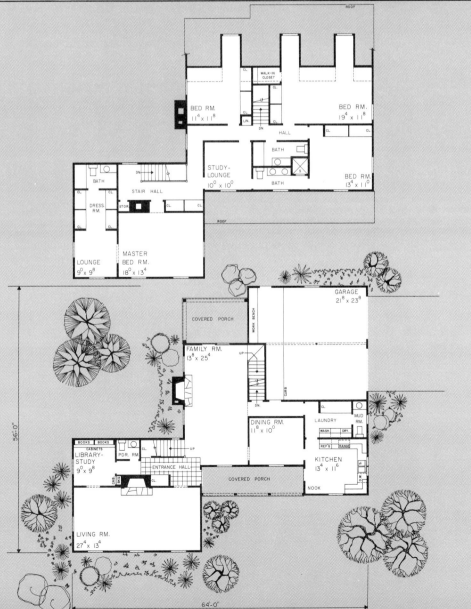

PLAN J2694

Type: Two-story
Style: Farmhouse
First floor: 2,026 square feet
Second floor: 1,386 square feet
Total: 3,412 square feet
Bedrooms: 3
Bathrooms: 2½ + washroom
Price schedule: C

This design is a beautifully up-dated version of the 18th-Century homestead of Secretary of Foreign Affairs John Jay. Our modern rendition offers great livability.

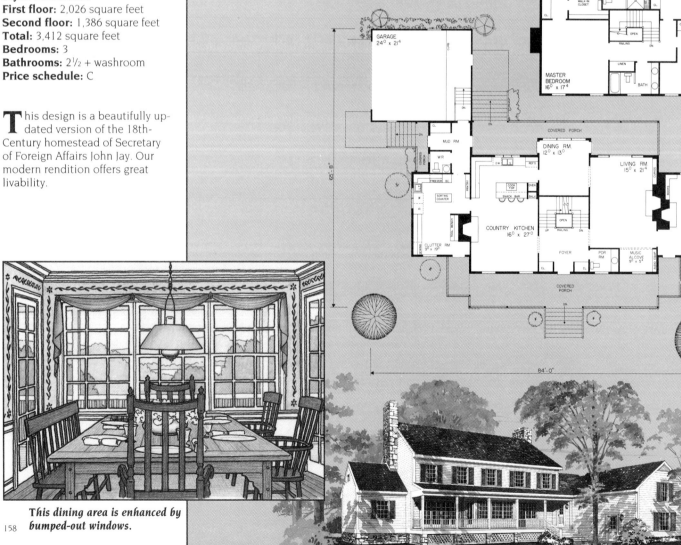

This dining area is enhanced by bumped-out windows.

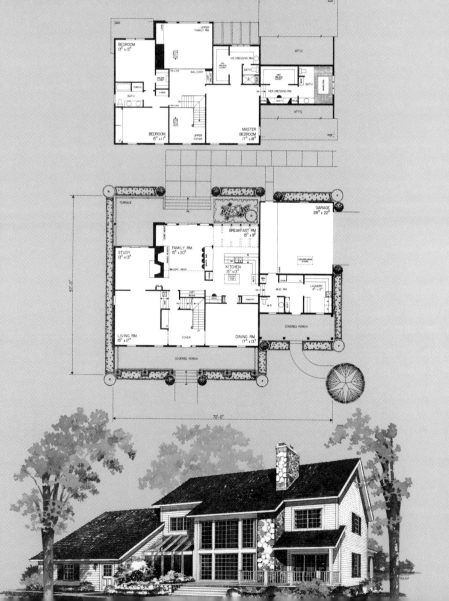

PLAN J2981

Type: Two-story
Style: Farmhouse
First floor: 2,104 square feet
Second floor: 2,015 square feet
Total: 4,119 square feet
Bedrooms: 3
Bathrooms: 2½
Price schedule: D

This formal two-story recalls a Louisiana plantation house, Land's End, built in 1857. The Ionic columns of the front porch and the pediment gable echo the Greek Revival style. Highlighting the interior is the bright and cheerful spaciousness of the informal family room area. It features a wall of glass stretching to the second-story sloping ceiling. Enhancing the drama of this area is the adjacent glass area of the breakfast room. Note the "His/Her" areas of the master bedroom, generous walk-in closets, and relaxing whirlpool spa. The wealth of terraces and covered porches adds great indoor-outdoor livability.

PLAN J2908

Type: Two-story
Style: Farmhouse
First floor: 1,229 square feet
Second floor: 1,153 square feet
Total: 2,382 square feet
Bedrooms: 4
Bathrooms: 2½
Price schedule: B

This Early American farmhouse offers plenty of modern comfort with its covered front porch with pillars and rails, double chimneys, building attachment, and four upstairs bedrooms. The first floor attachment includes a family room with bay window. It leads from the main house to a two-car garage. The family room certainly is the central focus of this fine design, with its own fireplace and rear entrance to a laundry and sewing room behind the garage. Disappearing stairs in the building attachment lead to the attic over the garage. The upstairs is accessible from stairs just off the front foyer. Included is a master bedroom suite. Downstairs one finds a modern kitchen with breakfast room, dining room, and front living room.

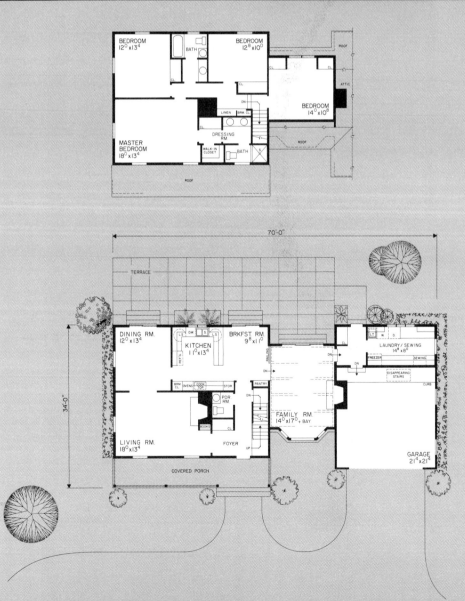

PLAN J2774

Type: Two-story
Style: Farmhouse
First floor: 1,370 square feet
Second floor: 969 square feet
Total: 2,339 square feet
Bedrooms: 3 or 4 (study)
Bathrooms: 2½
Price schedule: B

An all-time favorite design, this farmhouse includes the kind of features that appear on everyone's list: well-placed living and working zones, a wrap-around covered porch, three (optional four) upstairs bedrooms with two full baths.

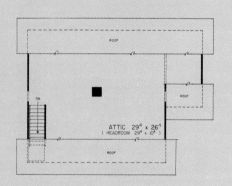

ROOF

ATTIC 29⁴ x 26⁴
(HEADROOM 29⁴ x 10⁴)

BEDROOM / STUDY 11⁰x13²

MASTER BEDROOM 13⁰x13²

BATH DRESS. RM.

VANITY

BATH

BEDROOM 10⁰x 10⁶

BEDROOM 13⁰x 10⁶

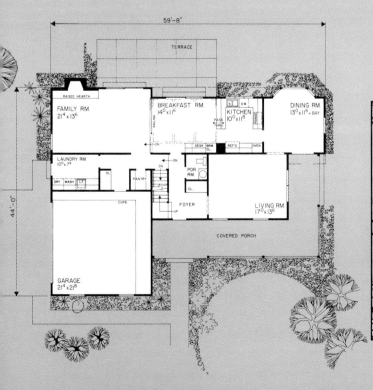

59'-8"

TERRACE

44'-0"

FAMILY RM. 21⁴ x 13⁶

RAISED HEARTH

BREAKFAST RM. 14⁰x11⁶

KITCHEN 10⁰x11⁸

DINING RM. 13⁰x11⁶ + BAY

LAUNDRY RM. 10⁸x 7⁶

DRY WASH LT.

PANTRY

PDR. RM.

FOYER

LIVING RM. 17⁰x13⁶

CURB

COVERED PORCH

GARAGE 21⁴x21⁸

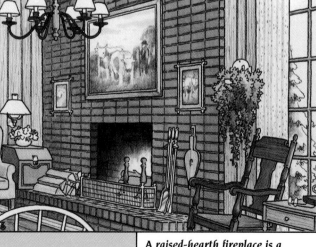

A raised-hearth fireplace is a glowing reflection of warmth.

PLAN J2664

Type: Two-story
Style: Farmhouse
First floor: 1,308 square feet
Second floor: 1,262 square feet
Total: 2,570 square feet
Bedrooms: 4
Bathrooms: 2½
Price schedule: B

Formal living on the left, informal on the right — that's the perfect configuration of this home's floor plan. And a country kitchen with island cook top serves both kinds of livability. Add to all this the two cozy fireplaces, a first-floor covered porch, a second-floor covered balcony, and a built-in bar in the family room and the picture is complete. The sleeping zone includes four bedrooms and two baths. Notice the walk-in closet in the master bedroom and twin vanities and window seat in the master bath.

A farmhouse living room is warm and inviting, with genuinely reproduced Early American details.

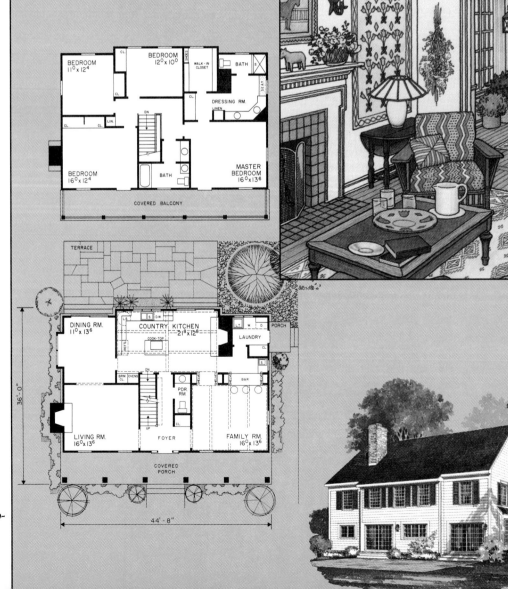

PLAN J1956

Type: Two-story
Style: Farmhouse
First floor: 990 square feet
Second floor: 728 square feet
Total: 1,718 square feet
Bedrooms: 4 (optional 3)
Bathrooms: 2½
Price schedule: A

Tremendous livability awaits the owner of this fine plan whether the choice is the four- or three-bedroom option. Blueprints for both plans are included in the purchase.

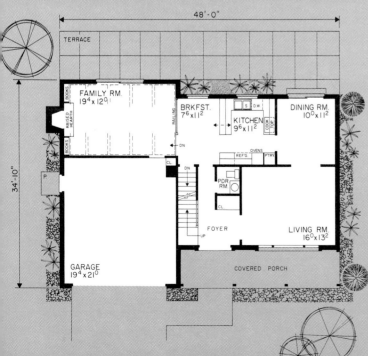

The charming double-door entry allows access to the living room.

PLAN J2890

Type: Two-story
Style: Farmhouse
First floor: 1,612 square feet
Second floor: 1,356 square feet
Total: 2,968 square feet
Bedrooms: 3
Bathrooms: 2½
Price schedule: C

This appealing farmhouse design is complemented by an inviting front porch, a nice-sized study, large family room, and efficient kitchen. A tavern/snack bar enhances entertainment options.

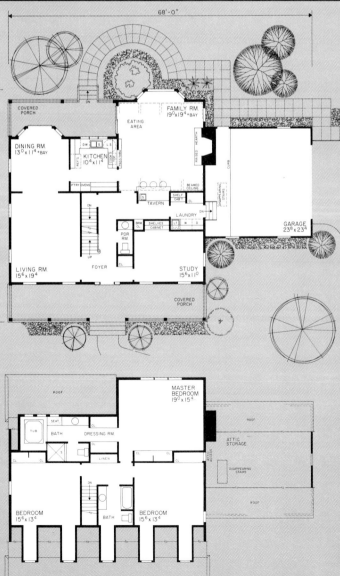

This family room is made special by a large bay window.

PLAN J2776

Type: Two-story
Style: Farmhouse
First floor: 1,134 square feet
Second floor: 874 square feet
Total: 2,008 square feet
Bedrooms: 3
Bathrooms: 2½
Price schedule: B

There is no lack of charm in this design, from the pleasing covered porch outside to a well-planned interior layout. A central entrance foyer directs traffic to a large living room and formal dining room with bay window. The nearby kitchen has a convenient pass-through counter to a family room with raised-hearth fireplace. In addition to a laundry off the service entrance, there is a powder room, well-located for guests to use. Upstairs are three bedrooms, including a master suite with walk-in closet, and two full baths.

The antique chandelier in this Colonial dining room will be used for softly lighting gracious dinner parties.

PLAN J2775

Type: Two-story
Style: Farmhouse
First floor: 1,317 square feet
Second floor: 952 square feet
Total: 2,269 square feet
Bedrooms: 4
Bathrooms: 2½
Price schedule: B

This farmhouse adaptation is characteristic of those found in the rolling hills of Pennsylvania. Its covered porches and impressive floor plan only add to the appeal.

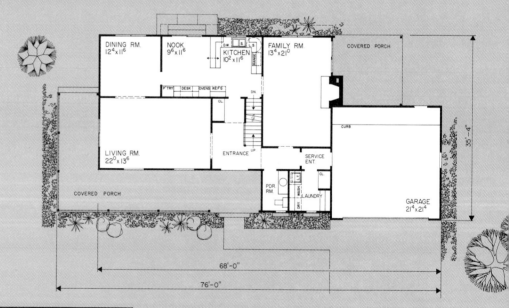

Sliding glass doors create the feeling of interior space in this room.

PLAN J2102

Type: Two-story
Style: Traditional
First floor: 1,682 square feet
Second floor: 1,344 square feet
Total: 3,026 square feet
Bedrooms: 4
Bathrooms: 2½ + powder room
Price schedule: C

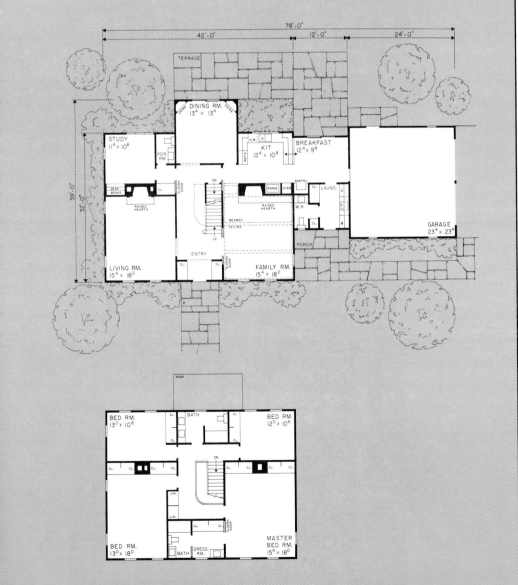

This Early Colonial adaptation has its roots deep in the past. While it is long on history, it is equally long on 20th-Century livability features. The narrow horizontal siding, appealing window treatment, exquisite door detailing, hip roof, massive chimneys and cupola are exterior architectural features which set the character. It would certainly be difficult by today's living standards to ask for more than what this floor plan offers. From the first floor laundry with its adjacent washroom to the study with its adjacent powder room, the interior is replete with convenient living appointments. There is a wealth of "little" features such as built-ins, raised hearths, pantry, pass-through to breakfast room, and beamed ceiling.

PLAN J1278

Type: Two-story
Style: Traditional
First floor: 1,336 square feet
Second floor: 1,080 square feet
Total: 2,614 square feet
Bedrooms: 4
Bathrooms: 2½
Price schedule: B

This inviting Early American design will be outstanding in any area. Note the uniqueness of the front covered porch entry to the family room. Interior features are many: U-shaped kitchen with pass-through snack bar in family room, cozy rear study, handy mud room with wash room, large living room with fireplace. There are four bedrooms upstairs, one with a built-in chest of drawers. The staircase is open to the entry hall below.

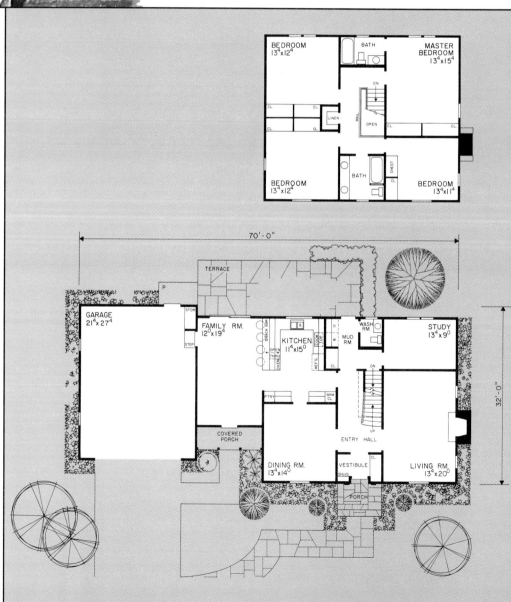

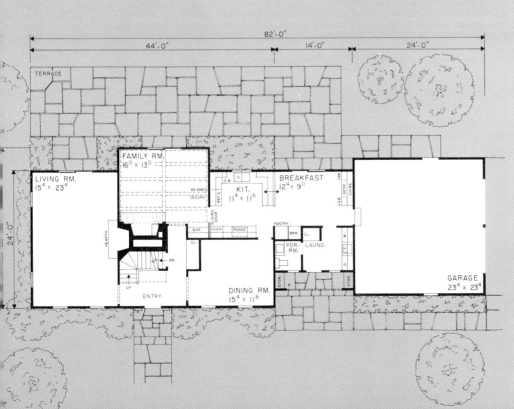

PLAN J2103

Type: Two-story
Style: Traditional
First floor: 1,374 square feet
Second floor: 1,056 square feet
Total: 2,430 square feet
Bedrooms: 3
Bathrooms: 2½
Price schedule: B

A wonderfully livable floor plan
awaits behind this engaging
traditional facade. On one side,
the large living room with fireplace and terrace access; on the
other, the dining room which connects to the kitchen/breakfast
area. At the center of things is a
well-appointed family room —
look for beamed ceilings, fireplace, bar, and sliding glass doors
to the terrace. The master bedroom on the second floor has a
large walk-in closet and bath with
double vanities. It shares this
floor with two family bedrooms
and another full bath.

PLAN J2870

Type: Two-story
Style: Traditional
First floor: 900 square feet
Second floor:
   467 square feet (left suite)
   493 square feet (right suite)
Total: 1,860 square feet
Bedrooms: 4
Bathrooms: 2½
Price schedule: A

This Colonial home was designed to provide comfortable living space for two families. The first floor is the common living area with all the necessities: living room with fireplace, formal dining room, breakfast room with snack bar through to kitchen, quiet study area. The second floor has two two-bedroom-one-bath suites. Notice that each of the smaller bedrooms has built-ins for economy of space.

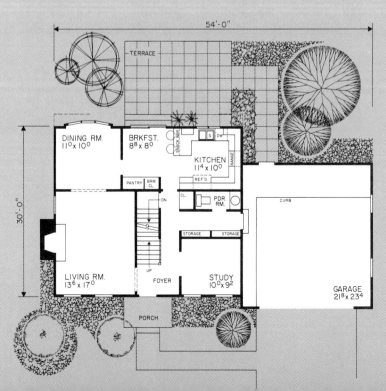

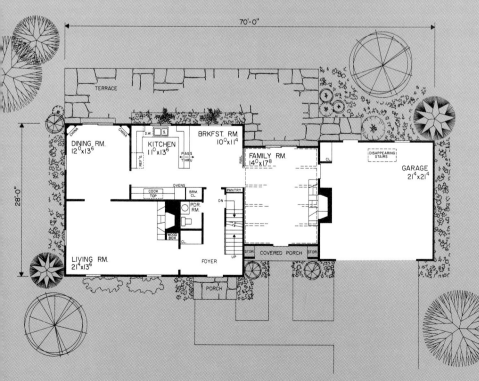

PLAN J2211

Type: Two-story
Style: Traditional
First floor: 1,214 square feet
Second floor: 1,146 square feet
Total: 2,360 square feet
Bedrooms: 4
Bathrooms: 2½
Price schedule: B

The appeal of this Colonial is sure to only improve with time. Its design will serve the growing family well. Besides the large living and dining areas, there is a beamed-ceilinged family room for informal gatherings. A U-shaped kitchen overlooks the rear terrace and has an adjoining breakfast room. The two fireplaces will be welcomed on cold winter evenings. Upstairs there are four bedrooms and two full baths. Each of the baths features double vanities.

PLAN J2921

Type: 1½-story
Style: Traditional
First floor: 3,215 square feet
   296 square feet (sun room)
Second floor: 711 square feet
Total: 4,222 square feet
Bedrooms: 3
Bathrooms: 2½ + washroom
Price schedule: D

Organized zoning by room functions makes this traditional design a comfortable home for living, as well as classic in its styling. A central foyer facilitates flexible traffic patterns. Quiet areas of the house include a media room and luxurious master bedroom suite with fitness area, spacious closets and bath, as well as a lounge or writing area. Informal living areas include a sun room, large country kitchen, and efficient kitchen with an island. Service areas include a room just off the garage for laundry, sewing or hobbies. Formal living areas include a living area and formal dining room. The second floor holds two bedrooms that would make a wonderful children's suite, with a study or TV area also upstairs.

The raised-hearth fireplace opens to a country kitchen.

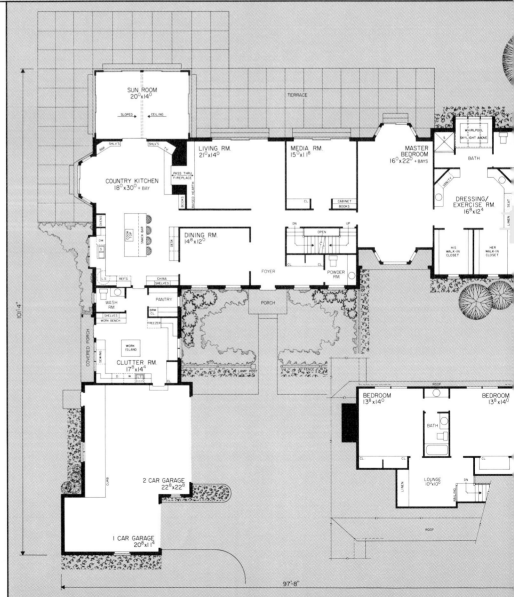

PLAN J1856

Type: Two-story
Style: Traditional
First floor: 1,023 square feet
Second floor: 784 square feet
Total: 1,807 square feet
Bedrooms: 3
Bathrooms: 2½
Price schedule: A

This small-sized Colonial offers much in the way of big-house features and livability. Some of its highlights are: separate living and playing terraces to the rear, two fireplaces — one in the family room and one in the living room, a service area with laundry and washroom, a two-car garage with storage. Upstairs there are three bedrooms and two full baths. Notice the charming exterior details: overhanging second story, shuttered windows, coach lamps.

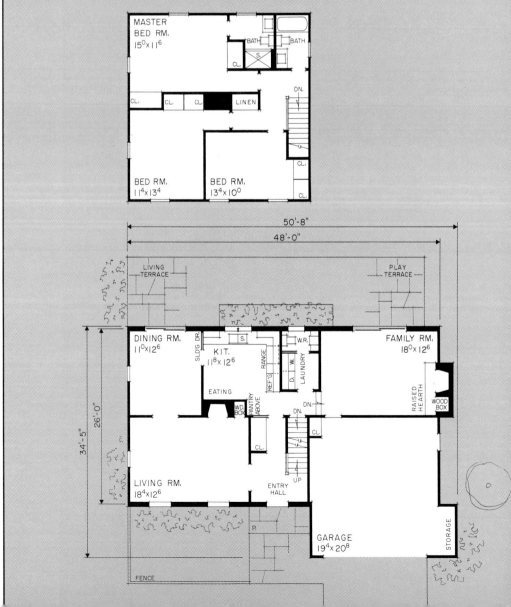

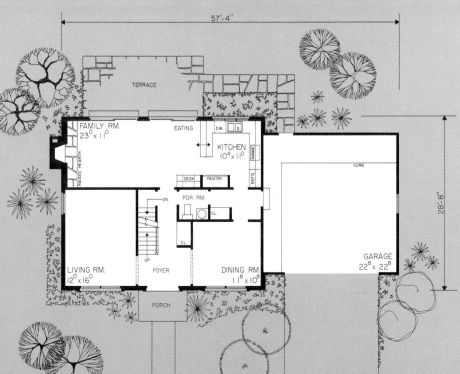

PLAN J2535

Type: Two-story
Style: Traditional
First floor: 986 square feet
Second floor: 1,436 square feet
Total: 2,422 square feet
Bedrooms: 4 or 5 (study)
Bathrooms: 2½
Price schedule: B

Here's an enchanting Colonial exterior encompassing plenty of interior livability. Past the double-door entry are formal living and dining areas flanking the foyer. A powder room just around the corner will accommodate guests. To the rear is a long, open family room and kitchen area. There's space here for informal dining and two sets of sliding glass doors lead to the terrace. Bedrooms number four or five depending on how options are chosen. Note the quaint dormer-style windows.

PLAN J2733

Type: Two-story
Style: Traditional
First floor: 1,177 square feet
Second floor: 1,003 square feet
Total: 2,180 square feet
Bedrooms: 4
Bathrooms: 2½
Price schedule: B

Perfect details accent the exterior of this Colonial home: shuttered windows, double coach lights, and wood and masonry siding. Inside there's a lot of livability. Notice how the family room is sunken and tucked out of the way. With a fireplace and terrace access, it's sure to be a favorite room. Other features include an L-shaped kitchen with island range and attached nook and a service area off the garage. Look for two baths and four bedrooms upstairs.

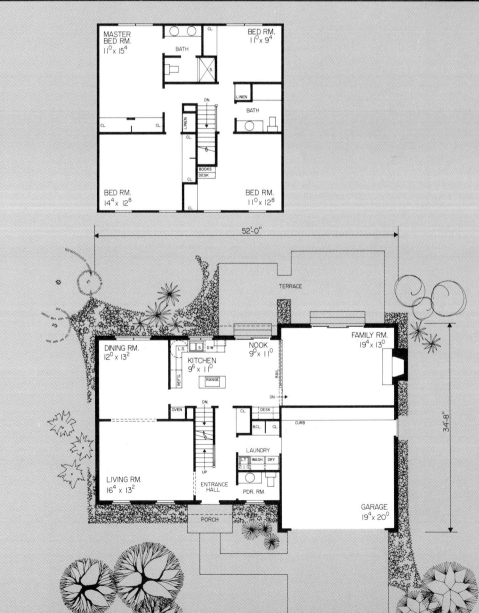

PLAN J2540

Type: Two-story
Style: Traditional
First floor: 1,306 square feet
Second floor: 1,360 square feet
Total: 2,666 square feet
Bedrooms: 4 + sitting room
Bathrooms: 2½
Price schedule: B

This efficient Colonial abounds in features: a spacious entry flanked by living areas, a kitchen flanked by eating areas, and, upstairs, four bedrooms including a sitting room in the master suite.

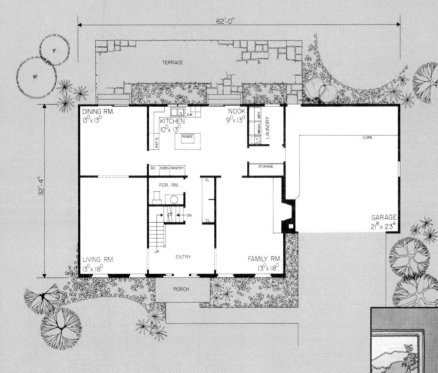

The family room hearth echoes the rustic stonework of the chimney stack.

177

PLAN J2598

Type: Two-story
Style: Traditional
First floor: 1,016 square feet
Second floor: 890 square feet
Total: 1,906 square feet
Bedrooms: 3
Bathrooms: 2½
Price schedule: A

In days of high-cost building, this relatively modest-sized two-story will be a great investment. The livable floor plan features a gracious entry with a curving staircase which leads to an enormous living room and a formal dining room. Adjacent to the dining room is a spacious kitchen with built-ins and an eating nook. Large windows in the nook and dining room provide views of the back yard; a sliding glass door in the living room leads to a terrace. Don't miss the separate laundry room off the kitchen. Three bedrooms upstairs round out the second floor. This compact plan will hold down the cost of construction while meeting the needs of today's family. Study this plan!

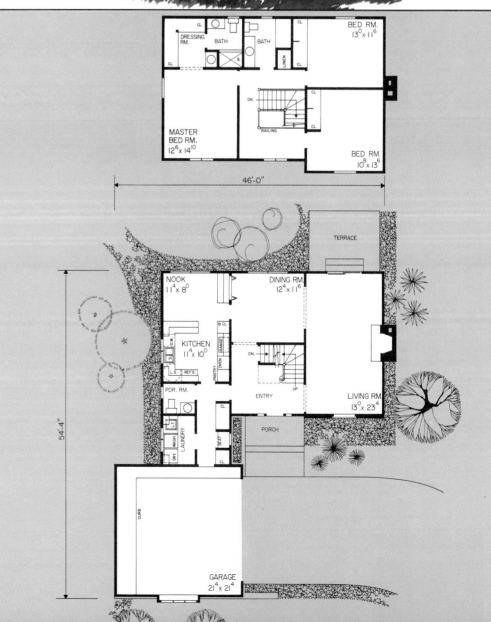

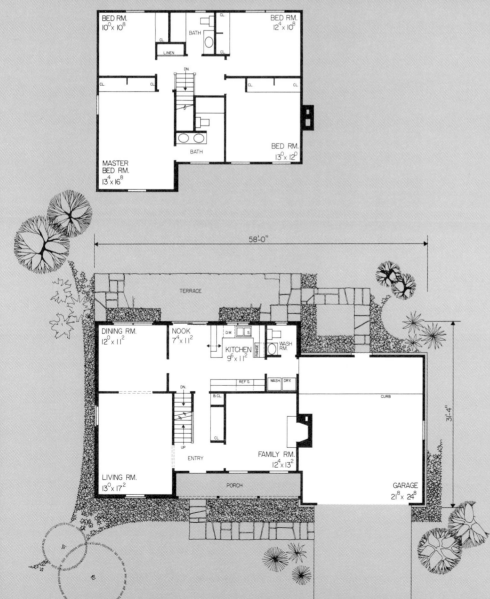

PLAN J2585

Type: Two-story
Style: Traditional
First floor: 990 square feet
Second floor: 1,011 square feet
Total: 2,001 square feet
Bedrooms: 4
Bathrooms: 2½
Price schedule: B

This design's elegant Colonial exterior is matched with a floor plan zoned for utmost livability. Left of the entry is the living room and connecting dining room making up the formal living zone. To the right of the entry is the comfortable family room for more informal occasions. The U-shaped kitchen serves the nook and is just steps away from the dining room. Also nearby is the laundry area and a washroom; an entrance to the garage makes short work of unloading groceries. To the rear is a large terrace for relaxing in the sun. Upstairs are four good-sized bedrooms, two full baths, and loads of closet space.

PLAN J2660

Type: Three-story
Style: Traditional
First floor: 1,479 square feet
Second floor: 1,501 square feet
Third floor: 912 square feet
Activities area: 556 square feet
Total: 4,448 square feet
Bedrooms: 5 + study
Bathrooms: 4½ + powder room
Price schedule: D

This elegant home is reminiscent of 18th-Century Charleston. A double-tiered porch overlooks the spectacular courtyard — a wonderful setting for outdoor parties. Also sharing this dramatic view are the formal parlor, dining room, and gathering room. To the rear is a spacious kitchen with breakfast room and a covered porch. The second floor features four large bedrooms and three full baths; the master boasts its own fireplace. The third floor houses a spacious guest room and a study. Don't miss the basement activities room and wine cellar.

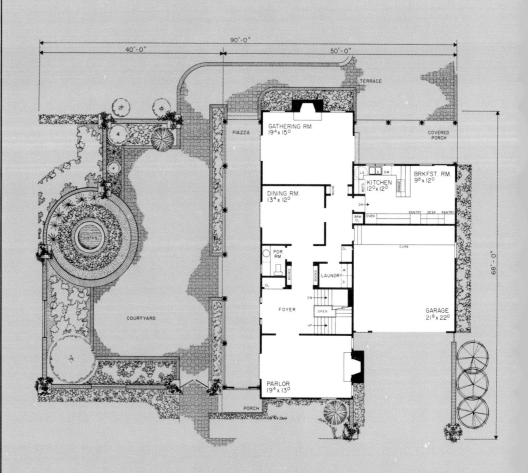

MASTER
BEDROOM
19⁴ x 13⁰

PIAZZA

ROOF

ATTIC

CL.

BATH.

S
CL.

BEDROOM
13⁴ x 11⁸

CL.
BATH

CL.

BEDROOM
14⁰ x 13⁰

DN

ATTIC

CL.

LINEN

ROOF

BATH

DN

ROOF

CL.

UP

BEDROOM
19⁴ x 13⁰

WALK - IN
CLOSET

GUEST
BEDROOM
11⁰ x 20⁶

ROOF

CEILING CLIP

CEILING CLIP

ROOF

BATH

LINEN

DN

STUDY
11⁰ x 13⁰

BASEMENT

WASH
RM.

GAME
STOR

WINE
CELLAR

UP

ACTIVITIES. RM.
17⁸ x 21¹⁰

PLAN J2599

Type: Two-story
Style: Traditional
First floor: 2,075 square feet
Second floor: 1,398 square feet
Total: 3,473 square feet
Bedrooms: 3 or 4
  (optional sitting room)
Bathrooms: 2½ + powder room
Price schedule: C

The massive fieldstone arch projects from the front line of this traditional two-story, providing a sheltered entrance. Inside, the foyer with its graceful, curving stair leads to the dining room, study, and family room. Adjacent is an L-shaped kitchen with an island range. The work area also includes a laundry room, washroom, and separate pantry. Contained in its own wing is the sloped-ceilinged, sunken gathering room. Notice the fireplace with its stone hearth. Upstairs are four large bedrooms; one of these can serve as an optional sitting room. The master bedroom features a dressing room with a separate vanity and abundant closet space.

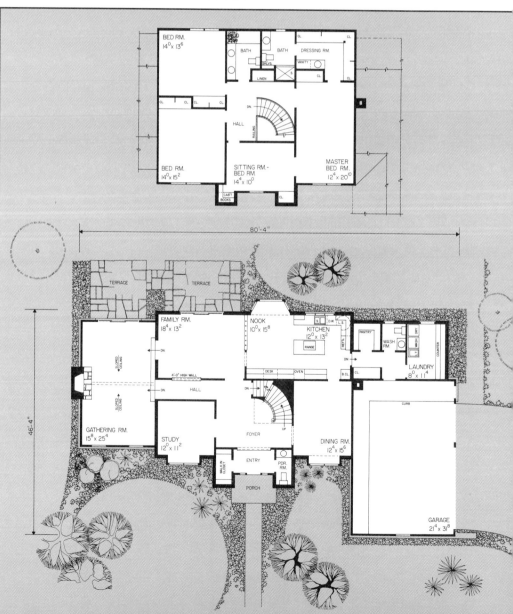

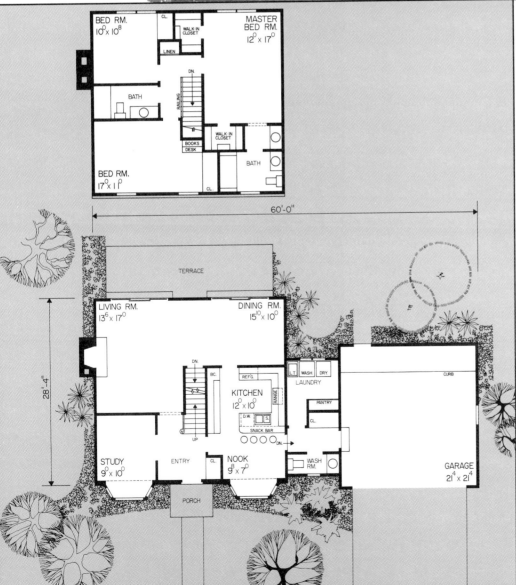

BED RM.
10⁰ x 10⁸

MASTER
BED RM.
12⁰ x 17⁰

CL.

WALK-IN
CLOSET

LINEN

DN.

BATH

RAILING

BOOKS
DESK

WALK-IN
CLOSET

BATH

BED RM.
17⁰ x 11⁰

CL.

60'-0"

TERRACE

LIVING RM.
13⁶ x 17⁰

DINING RM.
15¹⁰ x 10⁰

28'-4"

DN.

B.C.

REFG.

WASH DRY

LT.

LAUNDRY

CURB

KITCHEN
12 x 10

RANGE

PANTRY

D.W. S

CL.

SNACK BAR

UP

DN.

STUDY
9⁰ x 10⁰

ENTRY

CL.

NOOK
9⁸ x 7⁰

WASH
RM.

GARAGE
21⁴ x 21⁴

PORCH

PLAN J2558

Type: Two-story
Style: Traditional
First floor: 1,030 square feet
Second floor: 840 square feet
Total: 1,870 square feet
Bedrooms: 3 + study
Bathrooms: 2½
Price schedule: A

This relatively low-budget house is long on exterior appeal and interior livability. It has all the features to assure years of convenient living. The front entry leads to the study, to the living room and dining room, and to the kitchen. The spacious living room and dining room combination stretches the width of the house and looks out on the rear terrace and yard. The kitchen includes a snack bar and a nook. Notice the matching bay windows in the study and the kitchen. Upstairs are three bedrooms and two full baths.

183

PLAN J2622

Type: Two-story
Style: Traditional
First floor: 624 square feet
Second floor: 624 square feet
Total: 1,248 square feet
Bedrooms: 3
Bathrooms: 2½
Price schedule: A

Appealing design can en-velop little packages, too. Here is a charming, Early Colonial adaptation to serve the young family with a modest building budget. The plan features a living room with a fireplace and a sepa-rate dining room. A few steps away is a spacious kitchen with built-ins and an eating nook. There's a convenient entrance to the garage. On the second floor are three bedrooms and two baths. The storage area over the garage can be made into another bedroom, a nice option for grow-ing families. There's also an attic for additional storage space.

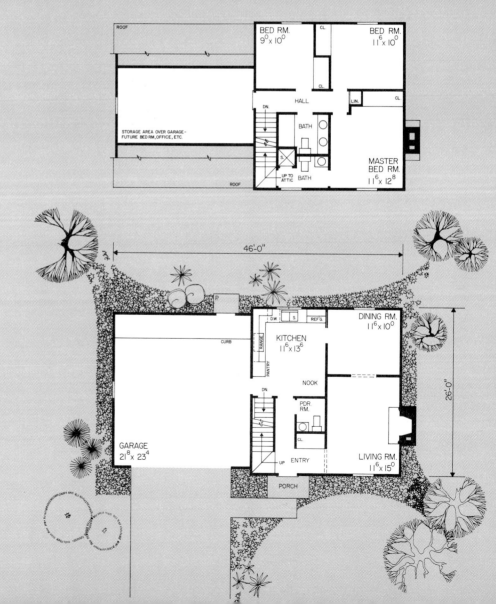

PLAN J2878

Type: One-story
Style: Traditional Ranch
Square footage: 1,521
Bedrooms: 2 or 3
  (optional study)
Bathrooms: 2
Price schedule: B

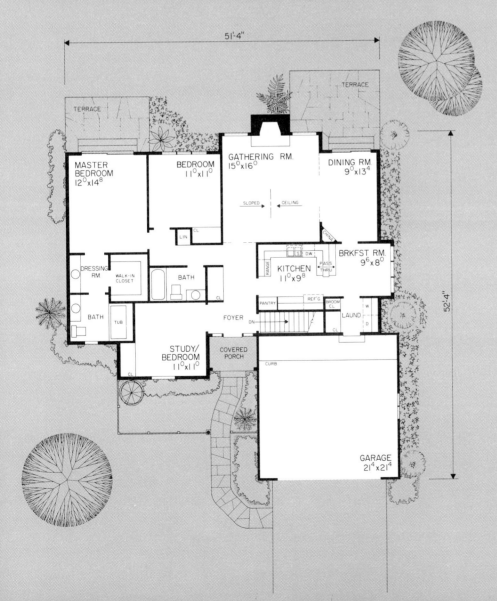

The efficient floor plan of this one-story makes optimum use of limited space. Ideally located, the sloped-ceilinged gathering room is warmed by a fireplace. The adjacent dining room has access to the rear terrace and is convenient to the kitchen. Also notice the corner china cabinet. The terrace off the dining room is a perfect spot for dining al fresco. Tucked away from the more active areas are two bedrooms. The master bedroom features a private terrace. The front study could easily serve as a third bedroom. This flexible plan is perfect for empty-nesters and small families.

PLAN J2880

Type: One-story
Style: Traditional Ranch
Square footage: 2,907
 (including greenhouse)
Bedrooms: 3 + media room
Bathrooms: 2½ + powder room
Price schedule: C

This comfortable traditional home offers plenty of modern livability. Off the foyer are the living room and media room with its built-in space for audio/visual equipment. The spacious country kitchen is a cozy gathering place for family and friends, as well as a convenient work area. A large greenhouse provides a cheery backdrop. Next door is the formal dining room. Three bedrooms include a large master suite with a whirlpool and His and Hers walk-in closets. Don't miss the clutter room! This multi-purpose work area features room for laundry, sewing, storage of tools, and greenhouse supplies.

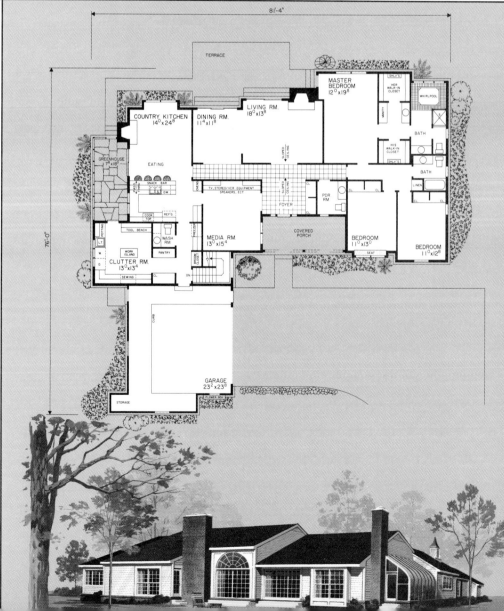

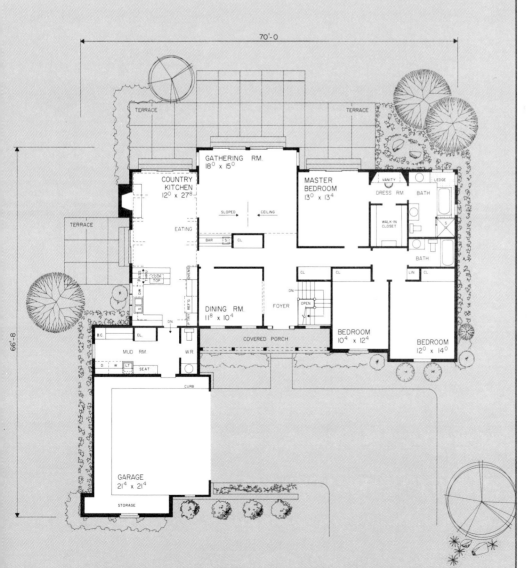

PLAN J2916

Type: One-story
Style: Traditional Ranch
Square footage: 2,129
Bedrooms: 3
Bathrooms: 2½
Price schedule: B

This traditional one-story features lots of comfort and livability. The foyer leads straight back to the spacious gathering room with its own wet bar. Next door is an enormous country kitchen with a U-shaped work area and an eating and living area with a fireplace. The dining room is conveniently close by. Away from bustle and noise, the sleeping area includes a master bedroom with a sumptuous bath. A large rear terrace, accessed by doors in the kitchen, gathering room and master bedroom, provides lots of outdoor living space.

PLAN J2707

Type: One-story
Style: Traditional Ranch
Square footage: 1,267
Bedrooms: 2 or 3
  (optional study)
Bathrooms: 2
Price schedule: A

Here is a charming Early American adaptation that is perfect for a small family or empty-nesters. The plan includes a living room with a raised-hearth fireplace, a dining room, a large kitchen, and two bedrooms with an optional third.

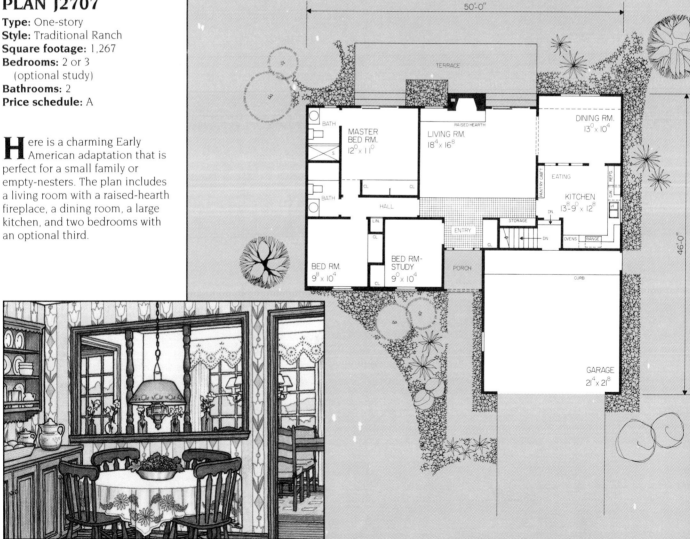

The kitchen features a pass-through to the formal dining room.

PLAN J2597

Type: One-story
Style: Traditional Ranch
Square footage: 1,515
Bedrooms: 3
Bathrooms: 2
Price schedule: B

A great starter or retirement house, this compact plan is a hardworker. The enormous, multi-purpose gathering room provides a large living and dining area. A sliding glass door to the terrace extends the living area outdoors in warmer months. There's an efficient kitchen with a nook. The sleeping area contains three bedrooms and two baths; the master has access to the terrace! Don't miss the storage area in the garage.

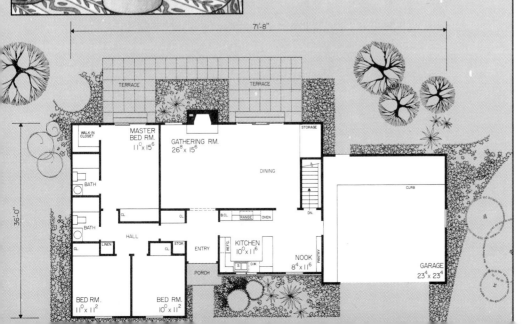

The spacious gathering room features a fireplace and overlooks the terrace.

189

PLAN J2888

Type: One-story
Style: Traditional Ranch
Square footage: 3,018
Bedrooms: 4 + study
Bathrooms: 3½
Price schedule: D

This distinctive home merges Early American styling with 20th-Century interior planning. There is space for every type of activity. The living room and dining room will take care of formal occasions; the study provides a quiet place to work. The flower porch is a sunny, cheerful haven. The spacious kitchen has loads of counter space and a peninsula cook top. For relaxing and informal entertaining, look to the family room. Notice the beamed ceiling, fireplace, and wet bar. The four-bedroom sleeping wing features a sumptuous master suite; notice the bow window and His and Hers baths and closets.

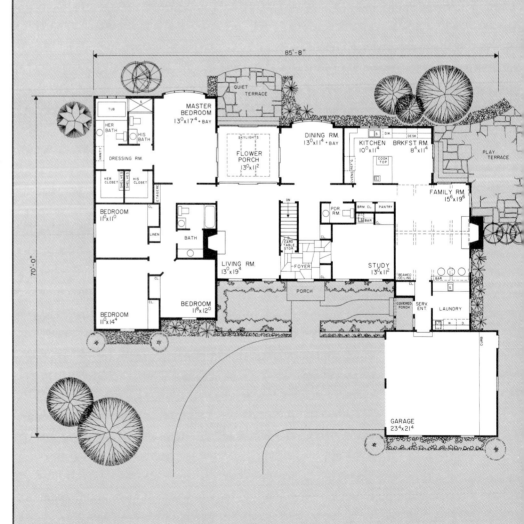

PLAN J2519

Type: One-story
Style: Traditional Ranch
Square footage: 2,889
Bedrooms: 3 + study
Bathrooms: 3
Price schedule: C

What a comfortable, livable home this is! A large, sunken gathering room is the centerpiece of the plan, leading into the dining room and study on either side. Next to the dining room is the kitchen and eating nook. Note the access to a terrace from each room.

Large windows flanking the fireplace flood the gathering room with natural light.

191

PLAN J1950

Type: One-story
Style: Traditional Ranch
Square footage: 2,076
Bedrooms: 3 or 4 (optional study)
Bathrooms: 2½
Price schedule: B

A delightful entry court welcomes visitors to this charming home. Inside, this spacious plan features a sunken living room which leads into the dining room — a nice arrangement for entertaining. Also notice the distinctive bow window. Nearby is the efficient kitchen with a pass-through to a breakfast nook. There's no shortage of built-ins and counter space. The beamed-ceilinged family room offers a spot for lounging. The private sleeping wing includes three bedrooms and an optional study. Notice the abundant closet space.

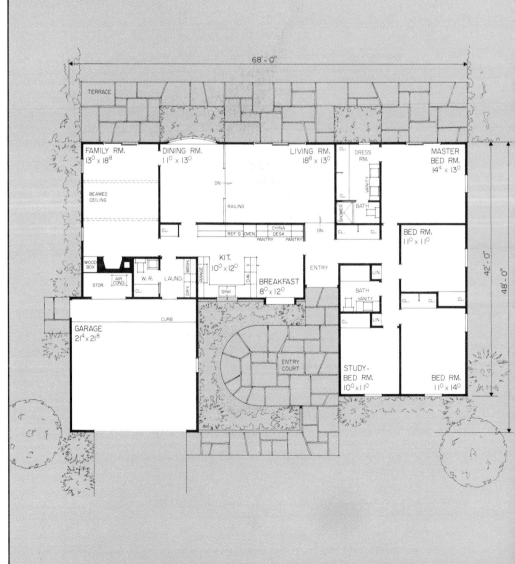

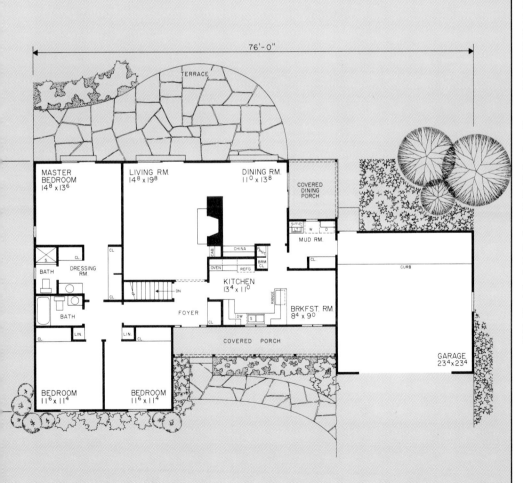

PLAN J2672

Type: One-story
Style: Traditional Ranch
Square footage: 1,717
Bedrooms: 3
Bathrooms: 2
Price schedule: B

This traditional ranch features an efficient, livable floor plan. The open living area promises comfort and practicality. A large fireplace separates the living and dining rooms without sacrificing open space. The large rear terrace will be perfect for outdoor parties or simply enjoying the sunshine. A covered porch off the dining room provides a spot for warm-weather dining. Nearby is the efficient kitchen with breakfast room. Three bedrooms and two baths in the sleeping wing round out the plan. Notice the storage space in the garage.

PLAN J2931

Type: One-story
Style: Traditional Ranch
Square footage: 1,998
Bedrooms: 2 + study
Bathrooms: 2
Price schedule: B

Little details make the difference. Notice the picket-fenced courtyard, carriage lamp, window boxes, muntined windows, and multi-gabled roof, to name a few. The interior is just as appealing. The sloped-ceilinged gathering room and study with fireplace provide formal and informal living space. Notice the wet bar in the gathering room. The dining room is conveniently adjacent to the efficient kitchen which has its own eating area and terrace for outdoor dining. Also notice the master suite with its dressing room, whirlpool, walk-in closet, and access to the terrace. You can't help but feel spoiled by this room.

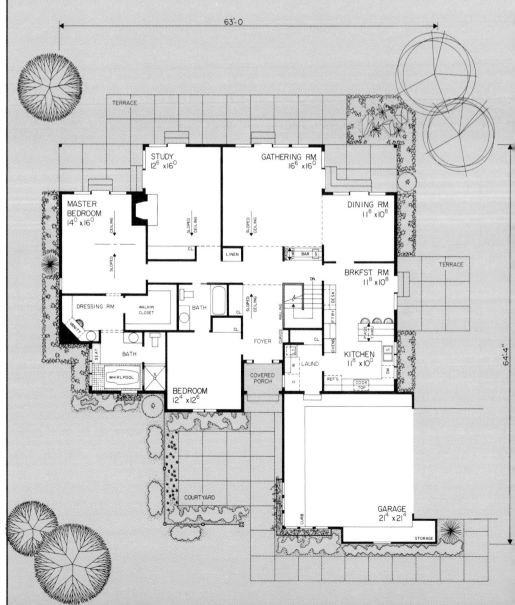

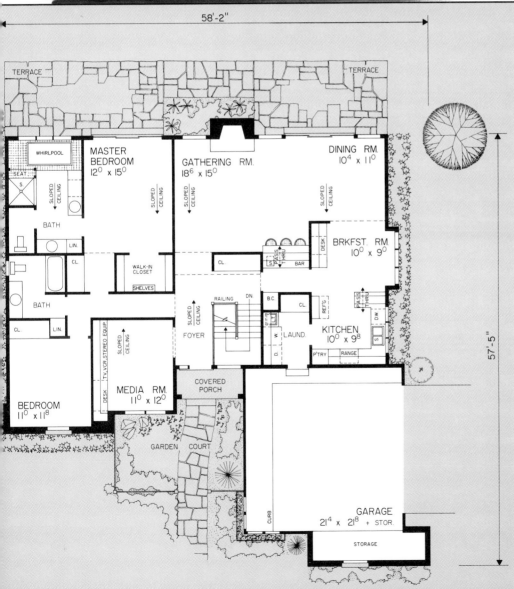

PLAN J2941

Type: One-story
Style: Traditional Ranch
Square footage: 1,842
Bedrooms: 2 + media room
Bathrooms: 2
Price schedule: B

Horizontal siding and field-stone lend an Early American feeling to this design. However, the modern interior leaves the old world behind. Immediately off the foyer is the media room for housing audio/visual equipment. Straight back are the open gathering room and dining room. Notice the sloped ceiling, fireplace, wet bar, and access to the terrace. A few steps away is the spacious kitchen and breakfast room. The sleeping area includes two nice-sized bedrooms. Notice the sumptuous bath in the master bedroom. This compact, elegant home is perfect for small families or empty-nesters.

PLAN J2261

Type: One-story
Style: Traditional Ranch
Square footage: 1,825
Bedrooms: 3
Bathrooms: 2½
Price schedule: B

This distinctive L-shaped home exudes traditional warmth and charm. Inside, there's lots of livability. The entry is strategically placed, leading to all areas. Placed off by itself, the living room is spared the wear and tear of cross traffic. The three bedrooms occupy their own private area. Also off the entry hall are the family room with beamed ceiling and fireplace and the formal dining room. The U-shaped kitchen is convenient to both and overlooks the backyard. Notice the terrace.

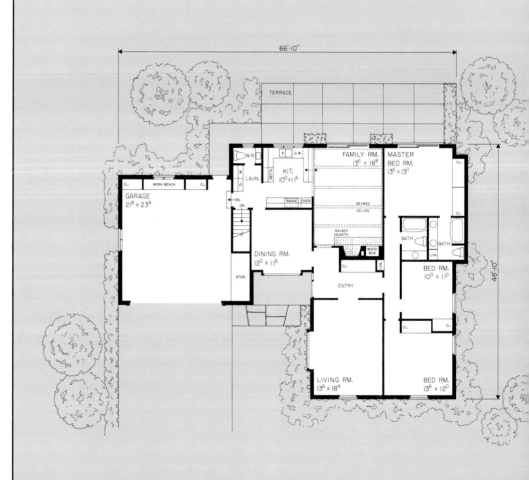

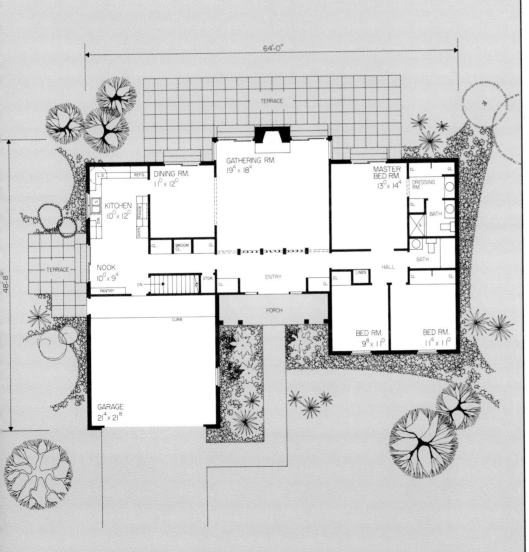

PLAN J2704

Type: One-story
Style: Traditional Ranch
Square footage: 1,746
Bedrooms: 3
Bathrooms: 2
Price schedule: B

The spacious gathering room with its fireplace and views of the back yard greets visitors in this charming home. Together with the adjacent dining room, these two rooms create a gracious entertaining space. The large terrace is a bonus space in warm weather. There's also a spacious kitchen and nook with its own private terrace for informal, outdoor meals. The entrance to the garage is convenient for unloading groceries. The sleeping wing features three nice-sized bedrooms; the master has access to the back terrace. Notice the abundant closet space throughout the house.

PLAN J2527

Type: One-story
Style: Traditional Ranch
Square footage: 2,392
Bedrooms: 3 + study
Bathrooms: 2½
Price schedule: C

Traditional styling combines with modern planning to create a comfortable, livable home. To the left of the foyer is a spacious kitchen with a bay-windowed nook. Adjacent is the formal dining room which is open to the sunken gathering room. Three bedrooms and a study complete the plan.

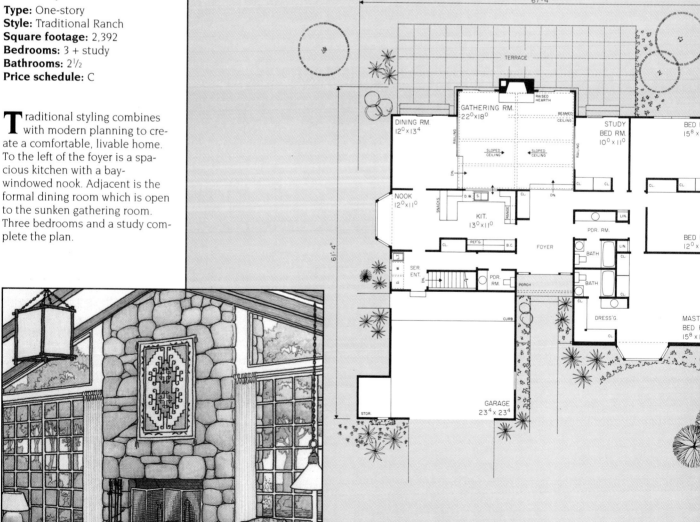

Sliding glass doors flank the stone fireplace in the gathering room.

PLAN J1829

Type: One-story
Style: Traditional Ranch
Square footage: 1,800
Bedrooms: 4
Bathrooms: 2½
Price schedule: B

All the charm of a traditional heritage is wrapped up in this U-shaped home with its narrow, horizontal siding, delightful window treatment and high-pitched roof. The massive center chimney, the bay window and the double front doors are plus features. Inside, the living potential is outstanding. The sleeping wing is self-contained and has four bedrooms and two baths. The large family and living rooms cater to the divergent age groups.

When You're Ready To Order ...

Let Us Show You Our Blueprint Package.

Building a home? Planning a home? The Blueprint Package from Home Planners, Inc. contains nearly everything you need to get the job done right, whether you're working on your own or with help from an architect, designer, builder or subcontractors. Each Blueprint Package is the result of many hours of work by licensed architects or professional designers.

QUALITY

Hundreds of hours of painstaking effort have gone into the development of your blueprint set. Each home has been quality-checked by professionals to insure accuracy and buildability.

VALUE

Because we sell in volume, you can buy professional-quality blueprints at a fraction of their development cost. With Home Planners, your dream home design costs only a few hundred dollars, not the thousands of dollars that custom architects charge.

SERVICE

Once you've chosen your favorite home plan, we stand ready to serve you with knowledgeable sales people and prompt, efficient service. We ship most orders within 48 hours of receipt and stand behind every set of blueprints we well.

SATISFACTION

We have been in business since 1946 and have shipped over 1 million blueprints to home builders just like you. Nearly 50 years of service and hundreds of thousands of satisfied customers are your guarantee that Home Planners can do the job for you.

ORDER TOLL FREE 1-800-521-6797

After you've studied our Blueprint Package and Important Extras on the following pages, simply mail the accompanying order form on page 205 or call toll free on our Blueprint Hotline: 1-800-521-6797. We're ready and eager to serve you.

Each set of blueprints is an interrelated collection of floor plans, interior and exterior elevations, dimensions, cross-sections, diagrams and notations showing precisely how your house is to be constructed.

Here's what you get:

Frontal Sheet
This artist's sketch of the exterior of the house, done in two-point perspective, gives you an idea of how the house will look when built and landscaped. Large ink-line floor plans show all levels of the house and provide a quick overview of your new home's livability, as well as a handy reference for studying furniture placement.

Foundation Plan
Drawn to 1/4-inch scale, this sheet shows the complete foundation layout, including support

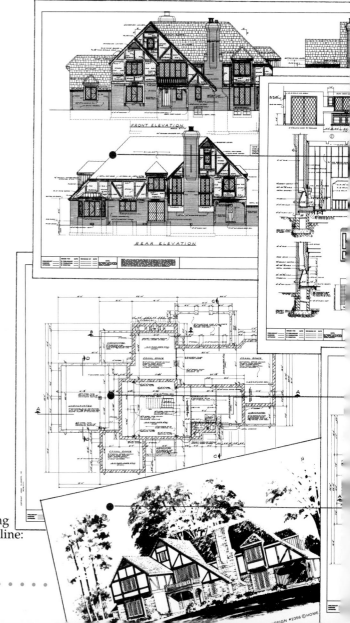

walls, excavated and unexcavated areas, if any and foundation notes. If slab construction rather than basement, the plan shows footings and details for a monolithic slab. This page, or another in the set, also includes a sample plot plan for locating your house on a building site.

Detailed Floor Plans
Complete in 1/4-inch scale, these plans show the layout of each floor of the house. All rooms and interior spaces are carefully dimensioned and keys are provided for cross-section details given later in the plans. The position of all electrical outlets and switches are clearly shown.

House Cross-Sections
Large-scale views, normally drawn at 3/8-inch equals 1 foot, show sections or cut-aways of the foundation, interior walls, exterior walls,

floors, stairways and roof details. Additional cross-sections are given to show important changes in floor, ceiling or roof heights or the relationship of one level to another. Extremely valuable for construction, these sections show exactly how the various parts of the house fit together.

Interior Elevations
These large-scale drawings show the design and placement of kitchen and bathroom cabinets, laundry areas, fireplaces, bookcases and other built-ins. Little "extras," such as mantelpiece and wainscoting drawings, plus moulding sections, provide details that give your home that custom touch.

Exterior Elevations
Drawings in 1/4-inch scale show the front, rear and sides of your house and give necessary notes on exterior materials and finishes. Particular attention is given to cornice detail, brick and stone accents or other finish items that make your home distinctive.

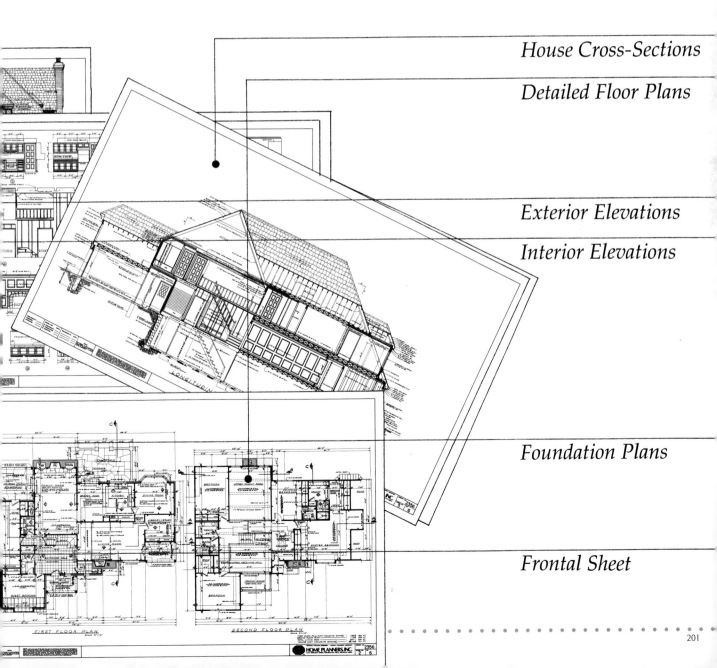

House Cross-Sections

Detailed Floor Plans

Exterior Elevations

Interior Elevations

Foundation Plans

Frontal Sheet

Important Extras To Do The Job Right!

Introducing six important planning and construction aids developed by our professionals to help you succeed in your home-building project.

To Order, Call Toll Free 1-800-521-6797

To add these important extras to your Blueprint Package, simply indicate your choices on the order form on page 205 or call us Toll Free 1-800-521-6797 and we'll tell you more about these exciting products.

MATERIALS LIST

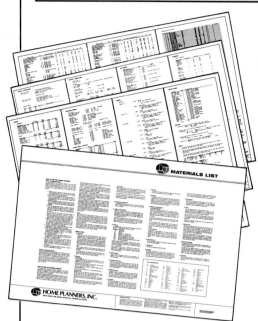

For each design in our portfolio, we offer a customized materials take-off that is invaluable in planning and estimating the cost of your new home. This comprehensive list outlines the quantity, type and size of material needed to build your house (with the exception of mechanical system items). Included are:

- framing lumber
- roofing and sheet metal
- windows and doors
- exterior sheathing material and trim
- masonry, veneer and fireplace materials
- tile and flooring materials
- kitchen and bath cabinetry
- interior sheathing and trim
- rough and finish hardware
- many more items

(Note: Because of differing local codes, building methods, and availability of materials, our Materials Lists do not include mechanical materials. To obtain necessary take-offs and recommendations, consult heating, plumbing and electrical contractors. Materials Lists are not sold separately from the Blueprint Package.)

This handy list helps you or your builder cost out materials and serves as a ready reference sheet when you're compiling bids. It also provides a cross-check against the materials specified by your builder and helps coordinate the substitution of items you may need to meet local codes.

SPECIFICATION OUTLINE

This valuable 16-page document is critical to building your house correctly. Designed to be filled in by you or your builder, this booklet lists 166 stages or items crucial to the building process.

For the layman, it provides a comprehensive review of the construction process and helps in making the specific choices of materials, models and processes. For the builder, it serves as a guide to preparing a building quotation and forms the basis for the construction program.

Designed primarily as a reference for the homeowner, this Specification Outline can become a legally binding document. Once it is filled out and agreed upon by owner and builder, it becomes a complete Project Specification.

When combined with the blueprints, a signed contract and schedule, the Specification Outline becomes a legal document and record for the building of your home. Many home builders find it useful to order two of these outlines—one as a worksheet in formulating the specifications and another to be carefully completed as a legal document.

Because local codes and requirements vary greatly, we recommend that you obtain drawings and bids from licensed contractors to do your mechanical plans. However, if you want to know more about techniques – and deal more confidently with subcontractors – we offer these remarkably useful detail sheets. Each is an excellent tool that will enhance your understanding of these technical subjects.

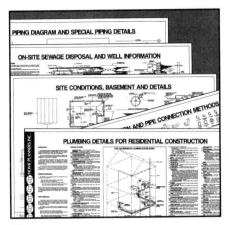

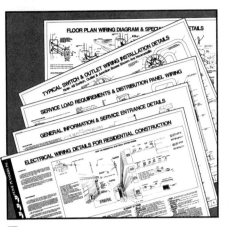

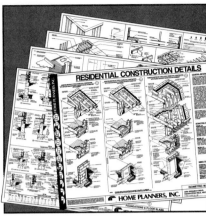

PLUMBING

The Blueprint Package includes locations for all the plumbing fixtures in your new house, including sinks, lavatories, tubs, showers, toilets, laundry trays and water heaters. However, if you want to know more about the complete plumbing system, these 24x36-inch detail sheets will prove very useful. Prepared to meet requirements of the National Plumbing Code, these six fact-filled sheets give general information on pipe schedules, fittings, sump-pump details, water-softener hookups, septic system details and much more. Color-coded sheets include a glossary of terms.

ELECTRICAL

The locations for every electrical switch, plug and outlet are shown in your Blueprint Package. However, these Electrical Details go further to take the mystery out of household electrical systems. Prepared to meet requirements of the National Electrical Code, these comprehensive 24x36-inch drawings come packed with helpful information, including wire sizing, switch-installation schematics, cable-routing details, appliance wattage, door-bell hookups, typical service panel circuitry and much more. Six sheets are bound together and color-coded for easy reference. A glossary of terms is also included.

CONSTRUCTION

The Blueprint Package contains everything an experienced builder needs to construct a particular house. However, it doesn't show all the ways that houses can be built, nor does it explain alternate construction methods. To help you understand how your house will be built – and offer additional techniques – this set of drawings depicts the materials and methods used to build foundations, fireplaces, walls, floors and roofs. Where appropriate, the drawings show acceptable alternatives. These six sheets will answer questions for the advanced do-it-yourselfer or home planner.

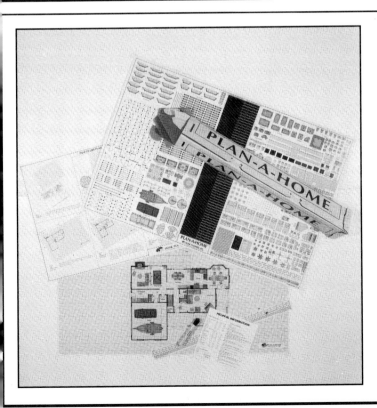

Plan-A-Home™

Plan-A-Home™ is an easy-to-use tool that helps you design a new home, arrange furniture in a new or existing home, or plan a remodeling project. Each package contains:

- More than *700 peel-off planning symbols* on a self-stick vinyl sheet, including walls, windows, doors, all types of furniture, kitchen components, bath fixtures and many more. All are made of durable, peel-and-stick vinyl you can use over and over.
- A reusable, transparent, *1/4-inch scale planning grid* made of tough mylar that matches the scale of actual working drawings (1/4-inch equals 1 foot). This grid provides the basis for house layouts of up to 140x92 feet.
- *Tracing paper* and a protective sheet for copying or transferring your completed plan.
- A *felt-tip pen*, with water-soluble ink that wipes away quickly.

With Plan-A-Home™, you can make basic planning decisions for a new house or make modifications to an existing house. Use with your Blueprint Package to test modifications to rooms or to plan furniture arrangements before you build. Plan-A-Home™ lets you lay out areas as large as a 7,500 square foot, six-bedroom, seven-bath house.

Price Schedule & Plans Index

These pages contain all the information you need to price your blueprints. In general, the larger and more complicated the house, the more it costs to design and thus the higher the price we must charge for the blueprints. Remember, however, that these prices are far less than you would normally pay for the services of a licensed architect or professional designer. Custom home designs and related architectural services often cost thousands of dollars, ranging from 5% to 15% of the cost of construction. By ordering our blueprints you are potentially saving enough money to afford a larger house, or to add those "extra" amenities such as a patio, deck, swimming pool or even an upgraded kitchen or luxurious master suite.

To use the index below, refer to the design number listed in chronological order (a helpful page reference is also given). Note the price index letter and refer to the House Blueprint Price Schedule at right for the cost of one, four or eight sets of blueprints or the cost of a reproducible sepia. Additional prices are shown for identical and reverse blueprint sets, as well as a very useful Materials List to accompany your plans.

House Blueprint Price Schedule
(Prices are subject to change without notice)

	1-set Study Package	4-set Building Package	8-set Building Package	1-set Reproducible Sepias
Schedule A	$150	$210	$270	$300
Schedule B	$180	$240	$300	$360
Schedule C	$210	$270	$330	$420
Schedule D	$240	$300	$360	$480
Schedule E	$360	$420	$480	$600

Additional Identical Blueprints in same order ......$40 per set
Reverse Blueprints ....$40 per set
Specification Outlines ....$5 each
Materials Lists
    Schedule A-D $35
    Schedule E $45

To Order: Fill in and send the Order Form on page 205 – or call us Toll Free 1-800-521-6797.

 Toll Free 1-800-521-6797

Normal Office Hours:
    8:00 a.m. to 8:00 p.m. - Eastern
    Standard Time
    Monday through Friday
    10:00 a.m. to 2:00 p.m. - EST Saturday

If we receive your order by 5:00 p.m. EST, we'll process it the same day and ship it the following day. When ordering by phone, please have your charge card ready. We'll also ask you for the Order Form Key Number on the opposite page. Please use our Toll-Free number for blueprint and book orders only.

By FAX: Copy the Order Form on the next page and send it on our International FAX line: 1-602-297-6219.

Canadian Customers

For faster, more economical service, Canadian customers should add 20% to all prices and mail in Canadian funds to:

Home Planners, Inc.
20 Cedar Street North
Kitchener, Ontario N2H 2W8
Phone (519) 743-4169

Before You Order . . .

Before completing the coupon at right or calling us on our Toll-Free Blueprint Hotline, you may be interested to learn more about our service and products. Here's some information you will find helpful.

Quick Turnaround

We process and ship every blueprint order from our office within 48 hours. On most orders, we do even better. Normally, if we receive your order by 5 p.m. Eastern Standard Time, we'll process it the same day and ship it the following day. Because of this quick turnaround, we won't send formal notice acknowledging receipt of your order.

Our Exchange Policy

Since blueprints are printed in response to your order, we cannot honor requests for refunds. However, we will exchange your entire first order for an equal number of blueprints at a price of $20.00 for the first set and $10.00 for each additional set, plus the difference in cost if exchanging for a design in a higher price bracket. (Sepias are not exchangeable.) All sets from the first order must be returned before the exchange can take place. Please add $7.00 for postage and handling via UPS regular service; $10.00 via UPS 2nd Day Air.

About Reverse Blueprints

If you want to build in reverse of the plan as shown, we will include one extra set of reversed blueprints for an additional fee of $40. Although lettering and dimensions appear backward, reverses will be a useful visual aid if you decide to flop the plan.

Modifying or Customizing Our Plans

With over 2,500 different plans from which to choose, you are bound to find a Home Planners' design that suits your lifestyle, budget and building site. In addition, our plans can be customized to your taste by your choice of siding, decorative detail, trim, color and other non-structural alterations.

If you do need to make minor modifications to the plans, these can normally be accomplished by your builder without the need for expensive blueprint modifications. However, if you decide to revise the plans significantly, we strongly suggest that you order our reproducible sepias and consult a licensed architect or professional designer to help you redraw the plans to your particular needs.

Architectural and Engineering Seals

Some cities and states are now requiring that a licensed architect or engineer review and "seal" your blueprints prior to construc-

tion. This is often due to local or regional concerns over energy consumption, safety codes, seismic ratings, etc. For this reason, you may find it necessary to consult with a local professional to have your plans reviewed. This can normally be accomplished with minimum delays, for a nominal fee.

Compliance with Local Codes and Regulations

At the time of creation, our plans are drawn to specifications published by Building Officials Code Administrators (BOCA), the Southern Standard Building Code, or the Uniform Building Code and are designed to meet or exceed national building standards.

Some states, counties and municipalities have their own codes, zoning requirements and building regulations. Before starting construction, consult with local building authorities and make sure you comply with local ordinances and codes, including obtaining any necessary permits or inspections as building progresses. In some cases, minor modifications to your plans by your builder, local architect or designer may be required to meet local conditions and requirements.

Foundation and Exterior Wall Changes

Most of our plans are drawn with either a full or partial basement foundation. Depending upon your specific climate or regional building practices, you may wish to convert this basement to a slab or crawlspace. Most professional contractors and builders can easily adapt your plans to alternate foundation types. Likewise, most can easily convert 2x4 wall construction to 2x6, or vice versa. If you need more guidance on these conversions, our handy Construction Detail Sheets, shown on page 203, describe how such conversions can be made.

How Many Blueprints Do You Need?

A single set of blueprints is sufficient to study a home in greater detail. However, if you are planning to obtain cost estimates from a contractor or subcontractors - or if you are planning to build immediately - you will need more sets. Because additional sets are cheaper when ordered in quantity with the original order, make sure you order enough blueprints to satisfy all requirements. The following checklist will help you determine how many you need:
_____ Owner
_____ Builder (generally requires at least three sets; one as a legal document, one to use during inspections, and at least one to give to subcontractors)
_____ Local Building Department (often requires two sets)
_____ Mortgage Lender (usually one set for a conventional loan; three sets for FHA or VA loans)
_____ TOTAL NUMBER OF SETS

O R D E R   F O R M

HOME PLANNERS, INC., 3275 WEST INA ROAD, SUITE 110, TUCSON, ARIZONA 85741

THE BASIC BLUEPRINT PACKAGE
Rush me the following (please refer to the Plans Index and Price Schedule in this section):

_____ Set(s) of blueprints for plan number(s) _____.	$_____
_____ Set(s) of sepias for plan number(s) _____.	$_____
_____ Additional identical blueprints in same order @ $40.00 per set.	$_____
_____ Reverse blueprints @ $40.00 per set.	$_____

IMPORTANT EXTRAS
Rush me the following:

_____ Materials List @ $35.00 Schedule A-D; $45.00 Schedule E	$_____
_____ Specification Outlines @ $5.00 each.	$_____
_____ Detail Sets @ $14.95 each; any two for $22.95; all three for $29.95 (save $14.90).	$_____

☐ Plumbing ☐ Electrical ☐ Construction
(These helpful details provide general construction advice and are not specific to any single plan.)

_____ Plan-A-Home™ @ $24.95 each.	$_____
_____ SUB-TOTAL	$_____

SALES TAX (Arizona residents add 5% sales tax; Michigan residents add 4% sales tax.) $_____

POSTAGE AND HANDLING	1-3 sets	4 or more sets	
UPS DELIVERY (Requires street address - No P.O. Boxes)			
•UPS Regular Service Allow 4-5 days delivery	☐ 5.00	☐ 7.00	$_____
•UPS 2nd Day Air Allow 2-3 days delivery	☐ 7.00	☐ 10.00	$_____
•UPS Next Day Air Allow 1-2 days delivery	☐ 16.50	☐ 20.00	$_____
POST OFFICE DELIVERY If no street address available. Allow 4-5 days delivery	☐ 7.00	☐ 10.00	$_____
OVERSEAS AIR MAIL DELIVERY Note: All delivery times are from date Blueprint Package is shipped.	☐ 30.00	☐ 50.00	$_____
	☐ Send C.O.D.		

TOTAL (Subtotal, tax, and postage) $_____

YOUR ADDRESS (please print)
Name_____
Street_____
City_____ State_____ Zip_____
Daytime telephone number (_____)_____

FOR CREDIT CARD ORDERS ONLY
Please fill in the requested information below:
Credit card number_____
Exp. Date: Month/Year_____
Check one ☐ Visa   ☐ MasterCard

Signature_____
Order Form Key   Please check appropriate box:
| TB18 | ☐ Licensed Builder-Contractor
        ☐ Home Owner

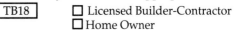

**ORDER TOLL FREE
1-800-521-6797**

205

Additional Plans Books

The Design Category Series

1.

ONE-STORY HOMES
A collection of 470 homes to suit a range of budgets in one-story living. All popular styles, including Cape Cod, Southwestern, Tudor and French. **384 pages. $8.95 ($10.95 Canada)**

2.

TWO-STORY HOMES
478 plans for all budgets in a wealth of styles: Tudors, Salt-boxes, Farmhouses, Victorians, Georgians, Contemporaries and more. **416 pages. $8.95 ($10.95 Canada)**

3.

MULTI-LEVEL AND HILL-SIDE HOMES 312 distinctive styles for both flat and sloping sites. Includes exposed lower levels, open staircases, balconies, decks and terraces. **320 pages. $6.95 ($8.95 Canada)**

4.

VACATION AND SECOND HOMES 258 ideal plans for a favorite vacation spot or perfect retirement or starter home. Includes cottages, chalets, and 1 1/2-, 2-, and multi-levels. **256 pages. $5.95 ($7.50 Canada)**

The Exterior Style Series

9.

330 EARLY AMERICAN HOME PLANS A heart-warming collection of the best in Early American architecture. Traces the style from Colonial structures to popular traditional versions. Includes a history of different styles. **304 pages. $9.95 ($11.95 Canada)**

10.

335 CONTEMPORARY HOME PLANS Required reading for anyone interested in the clean-lined elegance of Contemporary design. Features plans of all sizes and types, as well as a history of this style. **304 pages. $9.95 ($11.95 Canada)**

11.

TUDOR HOUSES The stuff that dreams are made of! A superb portfolio of 80 enchanting Tudor-style homes, from cozy Cotswold cottages to impressive Baronial manors. Includes a decorating section with colorful photographs and illustrations. **208 pages. $10.95 ($12.95 Canada)**

12.

COUNTRY HOUSES Shows off 80 country homes in three eye-catching styles: Cape Cod Farmhouses and Center-Hall Colonials. Each features an architect's exterior rendering, artist's depiction of a furnished interior room, large floor plan and planning tips. **208 pages. $10.95 ($12.95 Canada)**

Plan Portfolios

ENCYCLOPEDIA OF HOME DESIGNS
The largest book of its kind — 450 plans in a complete range of housing types, styles and sizes. Includes plans for all building budgets, families and styles of living.

14. 320 pages. $9.95 ($11.95 Canada)

MOST POPULAR HOME DESIGNS
Our customers' favorite plans, including one-story, 1 1/2-story, two-story, and multi-level homes in a variety of styles. Designs feature many of today's most popular amenities: lounges, clutter rooms, media rooms and more.

15. 272 pages. $8.95 ($10.95 Canada)

HOME PLANNERS' STYLE PORTFOLIO
A superb collection of today's most popular styles from Colonials to cool Contemporaries. Incorporates detailed renderings and floor plans with a Chronology of Styles and Glossary of Architectural Terms.

16. 320 pages. $9.95 ($11.95 Canada)

INDEX